Fusion or Fizzle

How Leaders Leverage Training to Ignite Results

UNIQUE
TRAINING &
DEVELOPMENT

Greg Schinkel

Irwin Schinkel

Fusion or Fizzle

How Leaders Leverage Training to Ignite Results

Library and Archives Canada Cataloguing in Publication

Leadership Training, Leveraging the Gains

ISBN 978-0-9734253-1-4 (print)

ISBN 978-0-9734253-2-1 (ebook)

1 Leadership 2 Management 3 Business 4 Human Resources 5 Training

Published by: Unique Training & Development Inc.

Contact Greg Schinkel

Unique Training and Development Inc.

http://UniqueDevelopment.com and http://FusionOrFizzle.com

E-mail gschinkel@uniquedevelopment.com

Printed in the United States of America

Table of Contents

Chapter 6: Best Practice Four

Chapter 7: Best Practice Five

Chapter 8: Best Practice Six

Chapter 9: Best Practice Seven

Section III

Chapter 10

Chapter 11

Dedications

This book is dedicated to:

God: the source of our natural abilities.
Our Lord: who taught us leadership by example.
The Spirit: that moves us to be caring leaders.

Our clients and participants:
who shared their concerns,
accepted new ideas and permitted us to revel in
the celebration of their successes.

Our families:
who have encouraged and
supported our efforts.

To you, our readers:
may this book be a source of insight and
inspiration and a contributing factor
in your continued career success.

Introduction & Overview

Congratulations on selecting this book. You have taken an important first step that opens a window on significant possibilities and potential for growth. Ideas and practices you find here should prove valuable throughout your career.

The Purpose of Fusion or Fizzle

Our extensive work as consultants and trainers taught us that too many organizations settle for too little in terms of actual change and measurable results from their training initiatives—essentially the initiatives fizzle out. What a terrible waste! These wasted opportunities result in frustration and disappointment. What strikes us is the fact that this waste is avoidable simply by making relatively few and inexpensive changes. These are detailed in the Seven Best Practices outlined in the following chapters.

This book has been written with your needs in mind: Its purpose is to share our experiences, practices and conclusions and do it in a way that provides the knowledge and confidence to apply the methods. Your current position may be at the executive, director, manager, supervisory or coordinator levels. It may be in functional areas such as operations, human resources, training, sales, finance or administration. Regardless of your role, the content in every chapter should prove helpful to you.

While reinforcing the importance of training methods, this book moves beyond these basics to focus on taking training for managers and supervisors to a higher level in terms of effectiveness and impact. *Fusion or Fizzle* is a guide to assist the reader in achieving two significant goals:

1. To show proof that training can be a significant catalyst in achieving the strategies and goals of the organization.

2. To equip these leaders with the ability to use management action to focus training efforts on high value, high payback,

high return opportunities within the organization and to boost the results by five or ten times or more.

Training should be viewed as a change agent and investment. As such it should generate measurable dividends as well as intangible benefits. That can and does happen in some organizations. In others it doesn't, and in some, no one seems to care. We sense that *you do care* and want to find methods and tactics to improve the outcomes of your training efforts.

A fundamental belief is that most employees, most of the time, do most or all of what is expected which leads us to ask, "Why then do organizations experience so many deficiencies in performance, processes, and products?" In response to this, you will notice that the book has two areas of focus:

- The primary focus is on the training and development of those in leadership positions: managers, supervisors and team leaders.

- The secondary focus is to share with leaders how they can improve the quality and outcomes of the training they provide to their staff to achieve drive real results.

Human resource and training practitioners struggle to justify their budget requests and complain of seemingly arbitrary reductions. Operating executives typically have one of these two perspectives: They either express disappointment in not seeing any meaningful change and impact from the investment in training. Or their expectations are too low, or non-existent in terms of expecting or demanding specific outcomes from the training. These issues are addressed in this book, and you'll see the overt and covert results from training that make it very cost effective. No matter where fingers are pointed, there is evidence that improvements are needed.

In our previous book, *Employees Not Doing What You Expect*, the twelve most frequent reasons employee performance does not meet our expectations were detailed. As we developed this content, it became obvious that in many cases the reasons were because those in a leadership role have not done what is expected and required. These leaders either do not know what is expected or how to do what is required. This deficiency inevitably erodes employee performance and eventually organizational results.

While researching this and the previous book we were struck by *the predictability of some problems.* It was obvious that most organizations experience their greatest difficulties, either when they have already introduced changes and find that the expected outcomes have not materialized or they are attempting to introduce change and find that employees are resistant and delaying implementation.

Change frequently triggers problems because during the planning phase, management plans for facilities, equipment, and software. It budgets the financial requirements but too often minimizes the funds provided for training and employee communications. The important human resource issues vital to implementing the plans are marginalized. In addition, experience has indicated that few organizations actually achieve the full gains possible from their training investment. Instead, they accept minor improvements and "feel good" reaction survey results as sufficient to justify the cost. This combination of low expectations, knowledge and skill deficiencies, lack of commitment, lack of application on the job and an absence of oversight contribute to the disappointing results.

Trainer/facilitators and HR leaders too often determine success solely through satisfaction ratings whether from management or the participants. Much more could have and should have been achieved but for the fact that one or more elements were lacking. Some trainers/facilitators prefer to ignore these issues, viewing them as being out of their span of control and responsibility. This degree of contribution requires a number of elements, which we will refer to as the **Seven Best Practices** described in Section II.

Finally, while senior executives struggle with serious business challenges and opportunities, these are rarely communicated to HR, the trainer/facilitators or course participants. There is no challenge or requirement to apply new knowledge and skills to one of the more important business initiatives.

> **There is an immense gap between executive strategies and priorities, and the actions being carried out by individuals at lower levels who are in the best position to make a meaningful contribution.**

Fusion or Fizzle offers Solutions

It is our goal to provide the practices and insights which will allow you to bridge this gap, to develop and enlist this pent up reserve of capable and motivated talent.

- In **Chapter One,** *When Leadership Training Is Not Done or Not Effective–Performance Deficiencies, Systematic Problems and Cascading Costs Occur* the impact and high cost of not training and the negative fallout that often results is highlighted. Here we also recognize that a company either invests in training as prevention or pays the costs of correction, which frequently are much greater and have a long lasting impact.

- In the **second chapter,** *Leadership Training Well Done– An Incredible Investment!* We share the stories of a number of small to large size companies and the gains they achieved not only in skills, but also in changed attitudes and gross margin and profit improvements.

- **Section Two** explores and emphasizes the *Seven Best Practices* that maximize the gains possible from leadership training. Each is highlighted in its own chapter with examples from many other companies. Throughout the *Seven Best Practices* section, we tell the story of Ovation Automotive a regional five-plant unit of a corporate entity with 26 plants world-wide. Chapter by chapter, we follow their efforts to establish training capability and conduct the initial leadership course at a time of innumerable problems. In each chapter their actions are compared to the related Best Practice and graded as **Grim, Good or Great or To Be Determined**. A few comments are added to explain the reason for the rating.

- **The last chapters provide a guide** for planning and implementing the Best Practices in your organization and illustrate how one multi-national organization applied the best practices and the results that occurred.

- **Forms and documents are provided** throughout the book and are available to download at FusionorFizzle.com. Use them as they are, or modify them to suit your needs.

When the term Unit Leader is used, it refers to those accountable for the performance of a designated group of people. It is used in place of such titles as CEO, president, owner, plant manager or department head or, in rare cases even, supervisor. The designation HR of course, refers to the head of human resources where actual titles may range from director of HR, VP of HR, manager of HR or HR coordinator.

To assist you in this journey, there are numerous anecdotes about actual situations. To protect the confidentiality of our clients we have changed the names of the companies and the individuals involved. However, the details regarding their needs, problems and challenges are factual. The results they achieved or didn't achieve are described as they were. There has been no effort to whitewash or gloss over the truth. We use these stories to illustrate the points and observations we've made. They also add flavor, build interest and sometimes entertain. Hopefully, they will generate in you the feeling of being there and experiencing the action and finally saying to yourself, "I could do that."

The book provides you with the opportunity to capture your thoughts and record them at certain points. You are encouraged to do so while the ideas and opinions are fresh in your mind. Then, prioritize those you intend to implement first. Begin with a few that are relatively fast and easy to do with a minimum of cost and within the limits of your budget and authority. Use the planning ideas in the last chapter as a starting point.

Finally, after you have read *Fusion or Fizzle* and have noted your ideas and intentions, keep the book nearby, so you will be prompted to glance through it again. There are so many aspects and nuances that no matter how often you read it, there is usually something more to be gained.

We hope that you will find it as useful, interesting and compelling as we have envisioned. Your comments and feedback are always sincerely welcomed. Please share with us which elements and ideas you found most useful and any additions you feel could be helpful for the next edition. Visit our website at FusionorFizzle.com.

Sincerely—the authors

Greg Schinkel and Irwin Schinkel

Section I

The two chapters in this section deal with these often debated questions:

- Is training worthwhile?
- Do the actual gains justify the costs?
- Why haven't we seen better results from the training we have done?
- What can we do to improve our results?

Chapter 1

When Leadership Training is Not Done or Not Effective, Cascading Costs Occur

The bottom-line is that when leaders are not effective, conflicts and costs increase and losses by omission result. These leaders tend to get stuck in the "blame game" by considering their customers, suppliers, the union, supervisors, or staff as possible sources for these losses. This diverts attention and energy from overcoming the actual root causes.

At Unique Training & Development, we've found through our years of extensive experience, that there is frequently a link between cascading losses and the lack of effective leadership training.

Clearly development for people in leadership positions is essential. Here are some of the losses that occur when these essential training needs are not addressed. You'll notice a box next to the loss indicator. Check off those now happening in your organization:

Manufacturing Organization Indicators

- ☐ Managers or employees are making negative comments
- ☐ Negative behaviors by managers or employees are increasing
- ☐ Conflicts between people becoming more serious
- ☐ Conflicts between departments (the silo effect) more entrenched
- ☐ Crises created by actions not taken are more frequent
- ☐ Crises created by inappropriate direct actions are growing
- ☐ Lack of co-operation and teamwork is evident
- ☐ Complaints and grievances are growing
- ☐ Health and safety violations are more frequent
- ☐ Late or faulty decisions delay actions
- ☐ Working to rule - work is not done or done late
- ☐ Absenteeism & tardiness up
- ☐ Errors, defects & omissions up
- ☐ Scrap and waste is increasing
- ☐ Rework and replacement costs are growing
- ☐ Shipping costs excessive
- ☐ Refunds and recalls up
- ☐ Production interruptions more frequent
- ☐ Throughput is restricted
- ☐ Overtime costs are increasing
- ☐ Customer complaints up
- ☐ Contracts and customers being lost

- ☐ Market share is declining
- ☐ Warranty costs are rising
- ☐ Image & reputation is declining
- ☐ Profitability is reduced
- ☐ Share value is declining
- ☐ Shareholder dissatisfaction is growing

> *(Note: Similar lists for service oriented and non-profit organizations are provided in the next chapter)*

INSPIRE

If you think education is expensive, try ignorance.

–Derek Curtis Bok, former President
at Harvard University

Early Indicators of Leadership Problems—Consider these as Opportunities for Improvement

People related problems are addressed eventually in all organizations. At times this is done quickly and in other cases completed only after disastrous problems force action. However, in many instances these issues are not seen as the root cause of the operational problems being experienced. Further, they are too seldom seen as the result of leadership deficiencies.

The elements listed above are examples of how the lack of training for leaders and those in authority impacts the bottom line. Actual problems are often evident much earlier in the overall process. They do exist, are known, are serious, are reported and they do impact the organization's overall performance. These problems contribute to higher costs and lower profits, but in some organizations they are ignored or tolerated until they worsen to the extent that they must be addressed.

But there is another important element that determines the extent of gains or losses. It is the fact that performance and effectiveness often depend on more than simply knowledge, skill, and application. It requires the removal of barriers that exist. The supply of necessary resources, timely decisions or something as simple as approval to proceed, all are beyond the control of the individual. These responsibilities reside with management and require that the Unit Leader take prompt and appropriate action. Again the question is, "Does that leader know what needs to be done and how to do it?"

From the leader's perspective, there is another way to look at it. Would an executive or manager take his vehicle to a dealer for servicing if he knew the employees were untrained? The same applies to the selection of a golf professional or financial advisor or a myriad of other service providers.

Yet, those same executives who deny the need for training for themselves and others are in the ultimate positions of influence and authority. Their lack of insight negatively impacts the quality of their products and services. (One likely contributing factor is that this occurs because Unit Leaders seldom interact with the customer and are rarely, if ever, required to deal personally with customer complaints.) It is about being stuck in the, "Problem, what problem?" syndrome. In fitting with this, it is essential to remember the following:

- What we tolerate, we propagate. It happens because we allow it to happen.

- Whether it is in quality, delivery, service or cost, the customer is **always** negatively impacted in some way by inadequately trained employees.

- Similarly, problems with suppliers are often the result of their employees and managers who have not been effectively trained. We suffer the costs and other consequences.

- Customers may not lodge a complaint; instead they simply buy elsewhere, providing no opportunity to rectify the problem. The resulting lost business continues until someone in authority realizes the losses and takes action. Then a costly correction is usually required.

Quality Is Free!

At one time, General Motors enjoyed almost 51% share of the automobile market in North America. In fact, some were calling for government intervention to limit the growth and size of the company. Now GM's market share is struggling in the area of 20% and it has experienced the unthinkable: bankruptcy protection. The Big Three, as they used to be called, have experienced huge losses and have restructured to drastically reduce costs. They began losing customers to off-shore manufacturers decades ago and it was on the basis of smaller, more economical vehicles and better product quality being offered by competitors.

When the Japanese automakers entered the North American market, they realized that quality was a problem for the Big Three and an opportunity for them. They invited American quality gurus such as Dr. Edward Deming, Dr. Joseph Juran, and later Philip Crosby to tour their plants, and advise them on quality improvement initiatives.

Deming became a Japanese hero and their government created the Deming Medal. They award it to companies who have best demonstrated his quality principles in action. Juran established his reputation with ideas and practices which emphasized top management involvement, the Pareto Principle, the need for widespread training in quality, the definition of quality as fit for use and the project-by-project approach to improvement. Crosby instilled the concepts of **Zero Defects and DRIFT (Do It Right The First Time)**. Two of his four quality principles were:

- The system for causing quality is not appraisal (inspection) but prevention.

- The performance standard must be zero defects, not, "That's close enough."

Crosby's book, *Quality Is Free*, became and remains a business bestseller. He also developed the term, "Cost of Quality" to encompass all of those costs which are incurred as a result of unacceptable quality, whether in a product or service. Crosby estimated that these costs often exceed 15% of gross *revenues*.

A few of those Cost of Quality elements that are sometimes overlooked are:

- Lost customers/lost business and the associated profits that should have accrued.

- Lost market share, which is costly to replace, if in fact this is ever possible.

- The cost of additional employees or overtime to respond to the volume of complaints.

- Lost sales of related products or services that are offered as a bundle.

- Reduced competitive advantage. In fact the lost business goes to a competitor who is stronger and more profitable as a result.

- Negative employee attitudes created by a constant bombardment of customer complaints and internal criticism.

Training Is Free And For The Same Reasons!

As companies experience the positive results of their quality improvement efforts, they became believers. Training related to quality issues increased, companies saw the value of becoming ISO 9000 certified. So impressed were the Big Three that they began insisting that their suppliers become certified as well. Next GM introduced their own, more stringent and broader standards: the QS 9000 series and insisted that suppliers conform. But the battle to convince managers of the benefits of prevention through training and other methods is ongoing, a challenge to all of those involved in delivery of leadership training.

> **The cost of training means that it is not without
> a price or fee. When training is planned and
> delivered with the focus on its financial benefit,
> the results most definitely outweigh the costs.**

Consider some North American and international examples where the value of training has been, or has not been realized.

From the U.S.A.: For those who were in New Orleans during hurricane Katrina the memory plagues them still. What also lives on is the reported failure of the FEMA director to rally and direct the rescue and recovery efforts. Republican Senator Trent Lott is quoted as saying, "FEMA was overwhelmed and undermanned and not capable of doing its job under the director's leadership." The director was replaced and some questioned the veracity of the information on his resume, which was used to justify his selection for the position.

From Canada: A national newspaper article was titled, "Train doomed from the start TSB report finds." The reporter begins her story by saying, "Outdated technology and poor training and supervision caused the derailment that spilled 40,000 liters of caustic soda into the Cheakamus River north of Squamish B.C. says a Transportation Safety Board report released yesterday." Further in the article, the corporate spokesman is quoted as saying that the rail company could not comment on the specifics of the report because of potential legal action due to the incident. Would you like to venture a guess as to how much this incident will eventually cost?

From Japan: Observers have attributed much of the Japanese corporations' success decades ago to its ravenous hunger for knowledge and its emphasis on training, bringing in foreign consultants and sending countless teams out to visit world centers where the most advanced knowledge was being pursued. Ironically, many Japanese companies now prefer for their training to be internal despite the value they received from listening to outside experts.

From India: A recent business article reported that, "Training and education cost Infosys $175 million dollars," then goes on to say, "Indian companies are convinced that upgrading the skills of their people is the way to win in a globalized world."

From China: This country is experiencing what Japan had previously experienced in recall costs, replacement costs and reputation damage. There have been recalls of hundreds of thousands of children's toys, toothpaste, tires and food products, just to name a few. The costs that Chinese producers, distributors and investors will suffer go far beyond the cost of replacing these items. The true costs should include the fact that North American consumers are becoming more reluctant to purchase certain goods with the "Made In China" label and are changing their buying habits. Training would have prevented much of this through the implementation of quality standards and practices.

Ensuring Training Success

When we look at the bigger picture, we see that problems and opportunities are two sides of the same coin. An opportunity not seized is a problem. A problem is an opportunity that is not being achieved. **Every problem is an opportunity for improvement and gain.** None should be ignored; they offer great potential. Too often problems are filtered, or hidden to avoid possible criticism. Unfortunately this distorts reality and delays pursuing a solution. In addition, it fosters a culture of denial.

For example, a local company went to great lengths to measure, report and minimize their cost of quality. Their reports indicated that this cost stood at about 3½% of revenues. When the participants in a training session were asked what *they* estimated the actual number to be, they said at least three times higher. Those potential gains were not being pursued.

Opportunities are never lost.

Competitors will seize those you miss!

They become stronger as a result.

Through our extensive work as trainers with a focus on development, we've found that there are two areas that a leader must be aware of before using training to prevent or solve workplace issues. One is an understanding of what training can and cannot do in the workplace and secondly, the reasons that training may fail and how to prevent it.

What Training Can—and Cannot—Do

1. Personality Issues: Training cannot inject personality characteristics lacking in an individual. It can, however, help develop interviewing and selection skills, which when applied, increase the likelihood that a more suitable candidate is recruited in the future. It can also change certain behaviors such as being more expressive or positive which may tend to enhance the person's ability to relate to others more effectively.

2. *Systemic Factors:* These factors are the roadblocks entrenched in organizations that impede success. Training itself cannot overcome procedural and process barriers to performance. It can often assist in developing the knowledge of how to identify these blockages and generate action to resolve them.

3. *Resources and Authority:* Training cannot by itself overcome a lack of vital resources, or authority to implement necessary changes. Yet, training can assist in identifying these needs. Then training in persuasiveness or assertiveness may be useful in influencing others of the need to make changes.

4. *Compensation and Rewards:* Related to systemic factors above, training cannot overcome a flawed compensation or benefit/reward systems that may be allowing, causing or contributing to employee dissatisfaction and negative behaviors. Once again, the training facilitator can provide her assessment and feedback regarding this situation to leaders who have the authority to correct the situation.

5. *Management Action/Support/Involvement:* Finally, the trainer/facilitator cannot insist, demand, or pressure participants to do anything. That is the responsibility of the leaders, the managers and supervisors who have the necessary authority to clarify and communicate expectations and, if not met, to confront and take corrective action. Training can inform, equip and provide the skills necessary to ensure such action is possible and done effectively.

Ten Reasons Training May Fail To Achieve Potential Gains

It is clear that training can be a key element to improving the bottom-line of organizations. Yet there are times when on the surface, the training provided seems not to have met expectations. Looking beneath the surface to secondary gains, results may be seen in abundance.

To possible negative experiences, here are ten reasons why training may not achieve expected potential gains:

1. **Low expectations by the Unit Leader** results in minimal personal involvement. Little is expected and therefore little is gained. Others involved quickly assume therefore that this is unimportant to the Unit Leader.

2. **The training is not linked to the organization's goals or strategies**; therefore it lacks perceived purpose. There seems to be no effort to connect the training to any specific application, project, or outcome, making it seem irrelevant.

3. **Participants are not briefed** by their manager/supervisor on why they have been enrolled in the training, how they will benefit or what they will be expected to do differently or better. Therefore, some are unmotivated, reasoning: "Why bother, the boss doesn't seem to care."

4. **The trainer/facilitator's methods (and/or materials) are inadequate or inappropriate** for some of these participants. Therefore there is a lack of credibility and/or connection with the participants and the person is simply, "a talking head," boring and ineffective.

5. **No one in management demonstrates any interest** in whether learning is taking place, whether the knowledge and skills are being applied, or whether anyone is gaining anything from the investment. This negatively impacts the participants and the facilitator/trainer and human resources people.

6. **A few participants are obviously and blatantly either making little or no effort** whatsoever or are distracting or otherwise undermining the learning of others and no one in management takes corrective action. This communicates the feeling that no one in concerned about what is happening. Often this same attitude and behavior is seen on the job where it is also ignored and finally becomes the culture of the organization.

7. **There are insufficient funds allocated to do the training effectively.** This affects everything from the

selection of the best facilitator, to the course duration, lack of pre-course interviews, lack of personal coaching availability, lack of progress reporting meetings with HR and management. Finally, those allied with the effort recognize the lack of support; frustration and de-motivation result.

8. **The training ends without celebration or recognition.** What could be a celebration of successful learning and on the job gains, a feeling of having accomplished something great, ends with a fizzle.

9. **There is no debriefing meeting, no reporting session, no measurement of gains** and no effort to determine how such activities could be made more effective in the future. This simply reinforces and perpetuates the negative attitudes, beliefs and perceptions that cause these situations.

10. **The training seems irrelevant to the participants.** It has been selected by the Unit Leader, HR manager or trainer/ facilitator because they participated elsewhere and found it interesting or because, it's the latest fad often referred to as "the flavor-of-the-month."

   Dynamic organizations rarely allow themselves to be hampered by past negative experiences. Instead they improve their skills, refine the process and try again.

When Training Is Not Done—Is It A Savings or Is It A Loss?

In the next chapter we learn about the problems at two companies, Green Bros. Concrete and Builder's Roof Truss Ltd. These stories illustrate that a lack of knowledge and skill by managers and not doing the training they require can be a serious cost to the company. Problems usually do not disappear nor just continue. They tend to escalate and as they do so, they cause increasing frustration, confrontation, blaming, lower productivity and a host of symptoms, many of which have been listed at the beginning of this chapter.

Application of These Ideas

The most significant ideas in this chapter for me were: _____
_____

As a result I intend to: _____

Action Prompt:

- Take a few minutes to review the second page of this chapter again. Check off those items that may indicate current or future problems.

- Review the "Ten Reasons Training May Fail To Achieve Potential Gains" and list those that seem to be present in your organization.

- Enter your intended future action in your daily planner.

Resources Available

Visit FusionorFizzle.com for a free Leadership Needs Assessment.

Chapter 2

Leadership Training Well Done— An Incredible Investment!

Training is usually considered only in terms of knowledge and skills gained. The true potential gain can often be much greater. To access these possibilities, we first have to open our minds. This may be difficult until we have tangible proof of the results. In other words, we have to believe before we attempt, and only then is it possible to achieve.

★ Nobody Has Ever Bet Enough on a Winning Horse

—Overheard at a race track by Richard Sasul

INSPIRE

The following three charts highlight the indicators for various organizations when managers receive training and subsequently are more effective.

Service Organization Indicators

Managers Not Effective	Managers Trained & Effective
Staff discourteous/disinterested	Staff capable, helpful and friendly
Staff lacks knowledge, unable to assist customers	Staff knowledgeable and able to assist customers
Dirty, disorganized facility	Facilities clean and tidy
Response slow/delayed	Customer response is as promised
Order, billing, shipping errors	Orders filled, promptly, correctly
Late or damaged shipments	Shipments made on time
Incorrect inventory	Inventory available when needed
Customer complaints	Positive referrals, recommendations
Customer service uneven, inconsistent	Customer service right every time
Equipment broken, unavailable	Equipment up to date and functioning
Customers lost	Customer base grows
Profits declining	Profits attractive/growing

Not-for-Profit Organization Indicators

Managers Not Effective	Managers Trained & Effective
Staff uncaring, rude	Staff capable and caring
Clients mistreated	Clients professionally treated
Furniture and equipment dirty and decrepit	Furniture clean and appropriate
Facility is dirty, disorganized	Facilities clean and well maintained
Inventory disorganized/missing	Proper Inventory is available
Funding ineffectively used	Funding effectively utilized
Mission unfulfilled	Mission achieved
Negative reputation in community	Respected in community
Donors disillusioned—reduced donations	Donors generous and supportive

Corporate Example—At the Local Level

One of the largest supermarket chains in the USA emerged from bankruptcy protection and closed or sold 500 stores.

Customers comparing two of their stores in the same Florida city have commented:

Managers Not Effective	Managers Trained & Effective
Shoppers periodically visit one of their nearby stores because of its convenient location. However, they say it has a 'dirty' odor, the stock is disorganized and scattered.	Shoppers say the same chain has a new store across the city from the first and here the shopping experience is totally different. It is clean, and orderly.
The employees are disheveled, uncaring, and unfriendly.	The staff are capable and considerate.
It could truly be said that performance here "stinks"*.	At this location, performance deserves a rating of 'splendid'.

Leadership deficiencies are often the root cause of both corporate and local problems. (*Shareholders detect a similar odor when they consider the erosion in their share value.)

Let's consider two specific situations where training lead to unexpected dividends. Though these examples relate to smaller enterprises, larger organizations can also be viewed as a series of smaller, self-contained business units.

A Concrete Fact: 600% Return On Investment!

Green Brothers Concrete Inc. is a small family business started by the father, who, with hard work and great determination, slowly grew it to seven employees. When he died unexpectedly, his sons Ed, age 22, and Peter, just 19, were thrust into the business. With little education, no experience and without warning, they built the business from dad's original 7 people to its present size of 28. There had been mistakes and setbacks, but shear determination and hard work was the catalyst for growth as it had been for their father. Now they were experiencing sleepless nights. The cause was a new product that was successful beyond expectations. Actually it was neither the product nor the customers that were causing the sleepless nights. The root cause was their inability to deal with the new employees being hired to ramp up production.

The Situation at Green Brothers Concrete Inc.: They realized they desperately needed new "how-to" abilities. Improvements were necessary in the process of interviewing, selection, hiring and training new people. The brothers admitted, "We are making too many mistakes in who we hire and how we get them started on the job. This is causing customer complaints, product returns and a lot of headaches."

The Solution: With some hesitation, they decided to reach out for training expertise, though uncertain as to their ability to select the most capable trainer. However, with that selection made, they were determined to make the most of the opportunity.

In deciding who should participate in the course, Ed, the president had given this some thought and said, "Both Pete, my brother and I will be in the group, plus our shop supervisor, our salesman and Betty, our bookkeeper/receptionist." When questioned about the inclusion of Betty as she had no direct reports, Ed responded with, "She's a leader around here because she makes things happen, she's important to our success and I've already talked to her and she has agreed to participate."

Ed may have had little formal education but he had intelligence, insight and wisdom. More than that, he had an attitude towards his people that fostered not only effort but loyalty.

Weekly evening sessions were held in the small lobby of their office area. The secret to their success wasn't dependent on the training facilities or equipment. It was the eagerness and dedication of the participants. While facilitating the sessions, we were learning as well, particularly how to translate corporate-gained management skills into doable and applicable small business on-the-job actions. This was not a situation for concepts and theories; rather it was a "Tell us what to do, why it's important and then show us how to do it." Even with Pete's resistance, there was never any doubt that they would begin to apply the next day what was discussed that evening.

Although training materials had been prepared in advance for use in the sessions, they quickly re-prioritized the sessions to deal with the most painful "felt needs" first. "In the past year," Ed began, "we have hired the wrong people. They either show up late or not at all. They do as little as possible and then too often do it wrong. Within a few weeks the good ones quit and go elsewhere for more money." The training needs were clear. "Let's get to the gold," Ed invariably directed. "The most urgent thing we have to learn is how to hire good people, how to train them quickly, and how to motivate them or cut them loose to find some other job."

Week by week, they learned, applied and gained skill and confidence. Rarely now would Pete challenge a suggestion. He had become a believer. Without specifically saying so, the success they experienced changed their perceptions about employees. Management was changing their actions, and this was in turn, leading the employees to change their own attitudes.

When the twelve weeks were over and the course completed, a final meeting was suggested to evaluate the benefits, payback and return on their investment. "Why bother doing that," Pete objected. "We know that we got our money's worth and that the training helped us."

But Ed in his quiet wisdom said, "I think maybe there is something more that we can learn, so let's do this on Friday morning." Just before heading back to work, they were given one final assignment, which had to be completed before the meeting.

As expected, Pete groaned and asked, "What is it?"

The Tangible Results: "Just bring a list of what you feel you gained from this training and prioritize it in terms of its importance," was Ed's reply. On Friday, Ed who is obviously a leader who leads by example, volunteered to go first. He said, "First on my list is the fact we finally learned how to find, interview, test for skills and do background checks on job applicants. With this change alone, we have cut our employee turnover by 90%." The others nodded in agreement.

"Can you put a price tag on that?" we asked Ed.

Ed responded, "That in itself is worth $50,000 to us because we spend less time on people problems and have fewer headaches."

Pete surprisingly spoke up and said, "Well I think that's worth a heck of a lot more, and I would put the figure at $100,000."

It was a passionate debate, which was finally ended by us saying, "Don't decide on the basis of emotion, think about it logically. Consider it on the basis of time, material and other actual savings." After further discussion they finally agreed that $25,000 was a conservative annualized number.

Now it was Pete's turn: "The most important thing to me was the list you gave us of steps to use when we train a new employee. Now we know what we're doing when we show a new worker how to do the job properly and safely."

"What's that worth to you and the company?" we asked. Pete obviously liked the number $100,000 because he offered it again and this time had support from the shop supervisor Tim.

Challenging them to think Ed said, "I personally find it difficult to believe that a list is worth $100,000 even if it were printed on banknote paper."

"It's not the list and it's not the paper," Pete shot back, thinking quickly he said, "the workers are making fewer mistakes and there are now seldom any repair jobs to do before shipment."

Ed encouraged, "Now you've got the idea Pete, those things can be and are measurable."

Pete said, "Excuse me for a minute or two and I'll be right back." In a flash he was back with a report. "The facts are scrap is down by 22% and rework, which we call patch jobs, are down by just a shade under 40%," he said with pride. "That means our labor costs are down and customer complaints are down," he added. "Isn't that worth $100,000?" he asked challengingly. (Pete had become a believer; in fact he had become a fanatic!)

On his notepad, Ed did some rapid calculating and answered, "Since we are being conservative, I'll give you a solid $50,000 for the year."

Beth who had been sitting quietly, said, "I guess it's my turn and I don't quite know what to say. All of the improvements have made my job easier. With fewer people quitting or being let go and therefore fewer hires, the paperwork is down. Since I handle customer calls, when there are fewer complaint calls, I can do other work. The only measurable things I can think of are that I don't have to work overtime any more and our paper usage is down somewhat. I'd put my number at $8,000." The group accepted Beth's number without question.

Finally, it was Dave's turn. "Since I'm responsible for sales, I can tell you my life is obviously easier now. My customers are happier with our product quality. I haven't gained any new customers yet but as word gets around and our reputation grows it can't help but work to our advantage. Why don't we just put down $10,000 for the potential new business we hope to gain?"

The team had turned into tigers, immediately vetoing that estimate saying, "When you show us actual sales numbers we will include them." They had learned. Using a flipchart, the **Costs** related to the training were listed as follows:

Trainer/Facilitator Fees	$7,200
Consumable Materials	1,500
Meeting Facilities	nil
Equipment Rental	nil
Participant Salaries/Wages	3,000*
Total	$11,700

*Some organizations do not include salary/wage costs in these calculations reasoning that the work normally done by participants is usually completed by them later or by someone else in the department at no additional cost. Others include these costs and add a factor for employee benefits as well. In this case, the participants were not paid for attending—they volunteered.

Using the information developed in the meeting, the estimated figures for the **Gains** were listed as:

Improved hiring & selection skills resulted in reduced management time spent in hiring, corrective counseling, discharge and replacement tasks. $25,000

Managers training new employees more effectively, resulted in reduced scrap and rework. $50,000

Reduction in time spent in recruiting, checking, and enrolling new employees—and less time spent responding to customer complaints. $3,000

Less cost for Admin. Asst. Overtime $8,000

Total $83,000

Some might point out that the numbers used were "guesstimates" which is true. Others would refuse to set such high numbers for the savings. Before using these numbers, management had already discounted them steeply from the original numbers suggested by the individuals. Finally, even if the figures were further reduced by half, the ROI would still be roughly 300%. An enviable gain!

Keep in mind, the older brother was the president and extremely careful in understanding his "numbers." His estimates were usually as accurate as if calculated to the nearest ten dollars. Calculating the number any finer would have been considered time wasted and of no additional value.

During the training, it became obvious that when Ed said little and had a slight smile it usually meant that he had a secret. This is something that the others hadn't noticed. In this case we both knew that when estimating the tangible benefits, no one had mentioned the improved productivity and the resulting increase in plant throughput. Ed knew. He understood the immensity of the benefits and the value to the company. But like many president/owners he liked to keep a little something in his back pocket for a future rainy day.

When leaving that day Ed shook hands and said, "We've learned much more than the course content. Now we realize that an investment in management and employee training can result in returns as great as those made in equipment, tooling and other hard assets. I will never, never forget this lesson." And he never has. For proof, simply visit his office where numerous course completion certificates proudly adorn his office wall.

Calculating Results: For those who may not be familiar with the term **Payback** or how it is calculated. Payback is how quickly the organization recovers the financial investment that has been made whether in facilities, equipment, software, etc. When funds are readily available companies may approve projects with a payback period of three years, or in some cases longer. If funds are limited they may reduce this to one year or as little as three months. This training generated gains of $83,000 as payback. Therefore, payback of the $11,700 investment was achieved in less than two months.

Return-On-Investment: (usually expressed as **ROI**) is simply the percentage of gain achieved on an investment, calculated over a one-year period. In this example the investment was $11,700 and the annualized gain $83,000 for a 600% return. By any standard this was an incredible investment. Consider the intangible gains simply a bonus. The anticipated increase in sales volume, simply considered a future bonus.

When calculating results, you need to include those that are *tangible* and those that are *intangible*. We have found that some only report tangible results and in others only the intangible results. The two are inextricably intertwined and both must be valued.

The intangible results at Green Brothers included a better work environment, fewer hassles, better co-operation, fewer conflicts and without a doubt, more positive attitudes, particularly in Pete's case. Are these important? Of course they are but can be difficult to quantify. The following lists are some examples of intangible and tangible gains.

The Gains—Intangible

- Managers learned effective hiring methods and used them at once. As a result hired more suitable, productive employees.

- Managers learned a step-by-step process for training employees.

- Managers were more confident and trained more effectively.

- Employees were competent sooner with better productivity and quality produced.

- Greater respect for "the bosses" who were perceived as taking time to train them.

- During the training sessions and on-the-job, greater teamwork developed: the result of learning, discussing and applying the methods at the same time.

- Fewer conflicts, hassles and headaches and better co-operation.

- Improved reputation regarding quality.

The Gains—Tangible

- Reduced management time spent on interviewing, hiring and replacing unsatisfactory people $25,000.

- Scrap down 22% and repairs were reduced 40%, a savings of $50,000.

- Less overtime for administrative assistant $8,000.

- Increased throughput and productivity and capacity.

- Reduced costs of material and labor.

- Fewer customer complaints and returns.

Observations: Some organizations make little or no effort to record the gains from training. Unfortunately, therefore, such gains are unknown and budgets too restricted and finally many opportunities for gains remain undiscovered, an unfortunate loss. On the other hand, a few organizations devote excessive time and effort to tracking gains. In fact, personnel at one national financial institution admitted that they devoted three days analyzing and reporting gains for each day of actual training conducted. This is too excessive.

Select a method that most easily generates numbers acceptable to the Unit Leader as being realistic. Often "guesstimates" by knowledgeable managers are sufficiently valid.

At Builders' Roof Truss—Two Spontaneous Discoveries

This story is about a discovery which we have termed spontaneous because no one involved was searching for gold. It was discovered while searching for simpler gains. This gold was two discoveries: the existence of a million dollar goldmine and the reality that financial figures can be fantasy.

The Situation at Builder's Roof Truss Ltd.: The vice president of Builder's Roof Truss Ltd. called requesting a visit to discuss their management and supervisory training needs. At the meeting, the president explained their situation. They were experiencing a surge in sales after a long recessionary period in the home building market. Having reduced their workforce, they now had begun hiring new people and promoting some plant employees to supervisory positions.

They identified the problem as being that these new supervisors were lacking in the know-how needed to be effective. Consequently, there were too many errors in production, too much scrap, too many late deliveries and too many customer complaints. (It sounded much the same as experienced by Green Brothers Concrete except that here they found fault with the supervisors.) This company too had been founded by the father, who unfortunately lacked the management skills and the financial resources to survive a deep recession. The company was forced into receivership. His two sons purchased the business from the receivers for a fraction of normal value but now they too were experiencing similar difficulty in achieving profitability.

To the credit of the brothers, Howard who became president and Evan who became vice president of sales, they promoted their most capable manager Art, to vice president of manufacturing. These three were in total agreement that they needed help and needed it quickly. All three said they would participate in the course and two weeks later the first evening session began.

The Solution: To generate discussion and participation a list of typical key result areas was presented. Participants were divided into two groups, one with Howard as the leader and Evan as leader of the second. The assignment was simple. Which key result area was most important to their company? Which should be number one? Was it profitability or customer satisfaction? Not surprisingly Howard's group chose *profitability* and Evan's group chose *customer satisfaction.*

After a few minutes of discussion in their separate groups, we reassembled and each brother made his arguments in favor of their choice. Howard, no doubt with his father's experience in mind said, "If we aren't profitable, we will soon be out of business and that's that."

Evan, as might be expected of the V.P. of sales had a persuasive comeback. He replied with, "Remember Howard, dad always said, look after the customer and the bottom line will take care of itself."

It would have been easy for Howard to react and say, "Look at where that thinking got dad." To his credit, he restrained himself. But the discussion continued on the topic of customer satisfaction, the competitive nature of the business and the increasing problems being caused by customers changing their orders, often just hours before scheduled production.

We refocused by asking, "How much do these changes cost the company in terms of scrap, redoing the work and slowing production?"

Without hesitation Howard replied, "It was $167,000 last year and that comes from our financial statement." The session ended with great participation but without further comments regarding costs.

The following week, on impulse we asked again. "What are all of these last-minute changes by your customers costing you?"

Impatiently Howard said, "I told you last week that it's $167,000." Once again the session ended and while all seemed well, something deep in our subconscious was troubling us.

The question was asked a third time a week later. This time with obvious sarcasm, Howard asked, "Do you have a hearing or a memory problem? I've told you twice before, the number is $167,000 right off our statements."

Apologetically I said, "I don't know exactly why, but something is troubling me. Please humor me and let's do a simple exercise. Howard, please take a blank sheet of paper and jot down the numbers the others are going to come up with."

The Results: Each manager in turn was asked, "What percentage of your department's time and effort is spent on redoing work?" The engineering manager answered 45%, the production manager said 40%, the sales manager mumbled 55%, and the bookkeeper admitted to 30%. Now we asked the president, "Knowing this information, what do you truly believe that these problems are costing?"

He answered quietly in a hoarse voice, "It's got to be costing us a million *!x#!* dollars a year!"

It was cruel but impossible to resist asking, "Those are pure profit dollars aren't they?"

He simply nodded, unable to comment in his state of shock. In fact, he couldn't and didn't participate for the balance of the session. It was as if some unseen miniature laser beam had inscribed the number $1,000,000 on the inside of Howard's eyeballs. At the end of the session he said, "It's much worse than I thought. We have our work cut out for us."

Howard's pursuit of that $1,000,000 was intense and relentless. It lasted at least five years. It included replacing his brother as V.P. of sales and his sister as the bookkeeper and countless other changes. Gains by the fifth year totaled in excess of $2,000,000. This enormous increase was not a direct result of our training session, but we ignited the realization of potential improvement which the training uncovered.

The Gains—Intangible

- During the training sessions and on-the-job, greater teamwork developed: the result of learning, discussing and applying the methods at the same time.

- The president and key managers learned the incredible value of training.

- When training was immediately applied they could see the rapid results.

- Realization that their approach to customer satisfaction was causing exorbitant costs and required a new approach.

- Learning that their numbers (and their bookkeeper) were unreliable.

- The way the training was done, everyone's participation and the skill of the facilitator resulted in realizing potential beyond expectations.

The Gains—Tangible

- Productivity and throughput were increased by 38% and customer order changes had been sharply reduced.

- Controlling customer changes reduced problems in every area on average by 65%.

- Supervisors effectively trained new employees creating better throughput and capacity.

- Fewer errors, which reduced scrap and replacement by 70%.

- Management team committed to continuous improvement and tabulated the gains monthly. (This is possibly the greatest gain.)

- With these improvements in conjunction with the newfound cost advantages and a favorable market, annual growth reached almost 25% (until the company was purchased by a larger company five years later.)

Training, at its finest, uses a synergistic combination of the facilitator's ability and experience with the participants' existing knowledge and applying them to actual significant opportunities within the company. What is the value of spontaneous discoveries? In this instance, more than a million dollar goldmine! Without the participation of senior management and their ability to implement changes promptly, and follow-up to ensure application, this important opportunity would have been lost. Every training activity should provide a method to capture report and implement spontaneous discoveries.

There are existing goldmines in every organization, regardless of size, location, products or services. The body of ore, the gold, may be small and difficult to locate, or large and just below the surface waiting to be extracted. Spontaneous discoveries happen when a problem is seen as an opportunity, and there is prompt corrective action to seize that opportunity. Management and the trainer/facilitator need to be partners. It is a collaboration that can produce great gains!

Words Recapture Lost Accounts

On a daily basis we are exposed to thousands of sound bites in an endless stream. The interaction may be for a few minutes or even a few seconds. These connections may be in person, on a cell phone or via email. The information may be useless or urgent. We often have less than a minute to evaluate the content, decide the speaker's intent and then determine how best to react. Not only do we have to do this in seconds but do it in a manner that is friendly, helpful and appropriate.

Organizations rely on such interactions to solicit new business or to respond to customer inquiries and do so in a way that ensures customer satisfaction, repeat business and an on-going relationship. Both profit-oriented businesses and not-for-profit social service agencies have this need. How effectively these brief encounters are conducted determines the success of the unit. A word may make the difference between a sale concluded or a sale lost; or of even greater importance, a new client gained or lost.

The Situation at Smile Dental Products: This successful distributor of dental supplies, for almost twenty years, had marketed directly to dentists and had grown over most of those years. But times had changed and with the entry of new competitors representing other manufacturers, the tide had begun to turn. In spite of a growing population base the company was losing clients and market share. Revenues had been declining for almost a year.

Brenda Baker, the sales manager called and at a subsequent meeting outlined the challenge and related concerns. "What we need help with," she began, "is to develop a two-pronged approach for use by our customer service people. Rather than simply accepting telephone orders from dental customers, we need our people to suggest other products and to mention special offers. In addition, when there are slack periods, we want them to call clients who haven't purchased in the past six weeks and mention special offers and new products and ask if they would like to try a sample." Management shared other concerns and it was important to the company's image that this be done in a way that was professional and sincere.

The Solution: For this client, a sales course was redesigned. All references to sales and selling were removed. Instead, it was re-titled: "Doing More for Our Clients—Making Helpful Suggestions Tactfully." Two weeks later the training was conducted, with a step-by-step process complete with useful words and phrases. Participants became comfortable with the initiative and returned to their jobs. Within a few days, Brenda called and said that when the service people were actually faced with the prospect of making their first calls, they panicked and asked for another session devoted totally to practicing their scripts. During the session, they asked the facilitator to demonstrate, role-play with them, critique as they practiced with each other, and then make actual calls in the presence of the group. The session didn't end until all agreed that, "We can do this!"

The Results: Within 90 days, sales revenues increased by 19% and 23 clients returned to do business with the company. The service people not only felt comfortable with their new roles, but saw themselves as proactive professional consultants assisting clients in their selection decisions.

Observations: Customizing course content rather than using off-the-shelf material can vastly increase effectiveness and the gains.

Practicing the right words is immensely more productive that practicing the *almost* right words, which could generate negative results.

The Right Words Drive Up Revenues

INSPIRE

The difference between the right word and the almost right word is the difference between lightning and a lightning bug.

– Mark Twain, humorist and author

How Important are the Right Words?

The Situation at Faster Lube: The challenges at Faster Lube were somewhat similar yet significantly different in one aspect. While they too needed to increase the size of each service sale it was not a telephone situation but had to occur in person. Moreover, it had to happen during those brief seconds after a customer drove their vehicle into the service bay. Currently, the store manager or assistant manager would approach and say, "What can we do for you today?"

Usually the customer would respond with, "Just a lube and an oil change." That's what happens 97% of the time," Dan Lennox, Regional Operations Manager, explained. "It's all over in a blink of an eye and we don't know how to bridge into a suggestion or a question," he added. Obviously frustrated, he said, "Our sales volumes are fine and we are profitable. The only way we can grow is to find a way to suggest additional services and do it in a way the customer will feel is helpful and do it within 60 seconds." He continued, "Fortunately, we know how well we are doing because we do random monthly telephone surveys. We know our sales per vehicle, the number of services sold, customer perception of sales pressure and finally customer satisfaction. As regional manager, I know what needs to happen but I'm stymied as to how exactly how to get it done. Between you and me," he confided, "getting this done and done right, could mean a bonus or a promotion for me and a lot more business for you folks." He dangled the incentive. Who could possibly resist?

In its 17 franchises and five company stores, the company employed primarily 16 to 25 year olds who served mostly 35 to 55 year old customers. There was a perception that this age difference caused customers to be less open to the suggestions of these younger people. Also relevant was the fact that the service people were primarily kinesthetic oriented and therefore they would learn best by doing and watching a demonstration rather than reading a manual.

The Solution: The first step was simple. Dan provided a card that listed current services. For additional information, one of our associates interviewed the employees at three of the locations and also interviewed a number of customers. It turned out that most of the customers enjoyed both the interview and being asked for their input, as did the employees.

A brief training workshop was developed and with it a CD that new employees could listen to in their cars and a DVD that managers could use for future training. Participants learned how to "read" customers more quickly and how to change their personal rate of speech and tonality to match those of the customer. They also used visual, auditory and kinesthetic methods to describe the most effective solutions. As you may have expected, sales increased from the very first day.

The Results: Dan did get his bonus and so did the employees. Of course, the company achieved higher revenues, greater productivity, and better margins, all of which flowed to the bottom-line.

Observations: Propagation of the methods to other units offered a significant multiplier in terms of gains.

Training materials that are specific and targeted need not be voluminous, in fact are more effective if they are sparse but specific.

Can Your Training Change Attitudes?

The Situation at Remark Electric Inc.: Linda, the HR manager at Remark Electric Inc. called to enroll three first line supervisors in an open leadership course. After providing the registration information, she paused and said, "Before these people attend, our plant manager Mike Lewis, wants to talk to the facilitator who will be conducting the training. I want to give you an opportunity to prepare for this meeting by telling you what his concerns are," she paused briefly to let that register, and then continued with, "He appointed Don, one of the guys from the shop floor, to a supervisory position about six months ago and he isn't happy with the result. Employees are complaining to Mike and me that Don comes across as arrogant, rude and uncaring. They say that they think the promotion has gone to his head, and as a result they are filing grievances, working to rule and generally dragging their feet to slow things down. Mike will ask whether your course can change Don's attitude and his behavior so that he can be successful as a supervisor," she concluded.

And, that is exactly the question Mike asked a few days later at our initial meeting. He was obviously frustrated and said, "Don was one of our best employees, always willing to take on any assignment; got along with everyone. I had high hopes for him and now this happens. It's as though he has had a personality conversion for the worse." He continued, "You know it reminds me of a story a friend once told me. A group of guys went hunting together every year to the same camp. The owner had a terrific dog named Worker. This dog would do everything—point and retrieve and never seem to tire. Then last year when they arrived at the camp, the owner told them that he had just changed Worker's name to Manager to reward him for his valiant service."

"Unfortunately, the first day in the field we learned that the dog named Manager now did nothing but bark incessantly and roll over to have his belly scratched." He grinned as he concluded the story and said, "I think the same bug has infected Don and I need help in changing this situation. Can you do anything to help me? Will the course change his approach to the employees and help him be more effective?"

We replied, "We can't change his approach and the course can't change him and you can't change him. Only he can change himself and he will only do that if he feels the need, wants to, and learns what to do differently and why. What we can do together, with the course is to provide the knowledge and skills, and then it's up to him."

The Solution: We advised Mike, "As plant manager it all begins with you. Before he attends the first session, sit down with Don and have a frank and friendly talk. Start by telling him why you promoted him. Be specific. Tell him the four positive behaviors that you just told me which earned him his promotion. Then tell him about what the employees are saying—without mentioning the names of the people. Tell him that you still believe in him and his potential to become a great supervisor. Then ask him what he finds easy about the job and what is giving him difficulty. When he mentions the employees just say, "Tell me more about that." When he finishes explaining say to him, "I just recently found out about a terrific and practical leadership course and plan to enroll a few people in it. Would you like to be one of them?" If he is the kind of person you and I think he is, his answer will be a positive one."

That is exactly what happened. Don seized the opportunity because he was motivated to learn and participate. All of the course content was relevant and the words and phrases fit well with his responsibilities. However, it was one assignment in particular that triggered almost immediate change. It required participants to initiate brief conversations with each employee everyday and in particular on Fridays and Mondays. There were suggested questions and friendly comments to develop a deeper knowledge about the employee and their interests. This personal approach created commonality and resulted in mutual respect, and co-operation.

The Results: Don said, "You know, I learned more about my employees and found that they are down to earth. They have many of the same interests as I do, as well as families and plans and dreams that aren't much different than those of my wife and myself. One of the guys is interested in classic cars which is also one of my interests. So now we have something in common to talk about other than the job." Don was effusive saying, "You folks and your help have likely saved my career."

Meanwhile, the employees were saying, "What happened to Don? He's been different lately. You know he's becoming a real human being. Once you get to know him, he's a great guy!"

Mike Lewis called to say, "This course has had a major influence on determining Don's future with us. But it's more that that," he continued, "his more positive behavior makes the work easier and more tolerable for every employee in his department. To give credit where credit is due, I have to say that these changes have also influenced the others we enrolled. The combined improvements have boosted productivity and reduced the number of complaints."

We answered by saying, "Take the credit Mike. You enrolled the people, explained to us what needed to be done, and you talked to Don in a way that motivated him to participate and apply what he learned. You also talked to each of the other participating supervisors at least once a week encouraging them to use what they were learning. By combining efforts, the needed results were achieved."

Finally, it was the fact that Don used the course methods and talked to his employees about their common interests. This changed both Don's attitudes and the attitudes of the employees. The "soft" or "people" skills resulted in fewer complaints and improved productivity. Soft skills often lead to "hard" results. It happens when the Seven Best Practices outlined in the following chapters are implemented.

Sales People Need Hard and Soft Skills for Success

Sales people are another example of the how hard and soft skills are needed for success. They require what is termed "product knowledge" which encompasses technical information about the product or service, how it is produced, delivered, used, and the benefits to the prospective customer. It is in communicating this information in a persuasive way that relates directly to the prospective or current client that can be termed soft or people skills.

Many sales managers have experienced the would-be sales person who has the appearance and the product knowledge, but lacks the ability to relate to the customer and to influence their buying decisions. Therefore, his or her career in sales is brief. The same can apply to supervisors, managers and executives.

Observations: Training done effectively, produces incredible results when the Unit Leader:

- Feels the impact of current problems personally.

- Sees their impact on others.

- Participates in the training sessions and ensures application.

- Sees the gain on the bottom line.

- To maximize the actual application of the training, changed behavior and results, the participant's manager should make time to speak with each person individually. And inform them of why they are being scheduled for training and what he or she hopes they will gain from it.

- Too often in training situations, the unit leader is MIA (Missing In Action) and this does not go unnoticed. The influence the leader has on participants cannot be delegated to the HR or training person. Influence is something the leader has and either uses or disregards to the detriment of the effort and the ensuing results.

- Training is always best when it is practical and assists the participants with tasks which they are actually required to perform, and where the results are measured and monitored.

- Time and effort spent in crystallizing what needs to be done, developing practical content and appropriate learning methods maximizes effectiveness and pay-offs with measurable dividends.

- Participants in training sessions are frustrated when the facilitator lectures about concepts, philosophies and theories, while limiting time available for discussion of practical application.

- Great benefits can accrue from a few words aptly chosen and carefully used.

- Astute leaders insist on knowing both the tangible and intangible results for their training investment. Once they experience the tangible, they seldom ask, "How little do we have to spend?" or "How long can we delay this?" but start asking questions such as, "What do we need to invest to achieve maximum returns, how soon can we get started, how will the results be calculated and reported, and how do you want me to be involved?"

> The greatest discovery of my generation is that human beings can alter their lives by altering their attitude of mind.
>
> *–William James, Psychologist*

Researchers have also learned that frequently, a change in behavior occurs first, followed by a change in attitudes.

One or More of These Gains are Possible

Here are some ways for you to look at what "gains" means in a more comprehensive way. This approach captures both long and short-term gains as well as tangible and intangible ones. Know that with all training done, one or more of these gains are possible—and in some cases all are achievable.

Immediate Once-Only Savings: This applies to those savings achieved on a one-time basis for a specific project, a single customer, or single location.

Cascading Gains: Often there is a cascading flow of benefits when managers and employees apply new skills. In an earlier example, this was demonstrated through improving the hiring, interviewing and selection skills combined with enhancing job instruction methods (which reduced scrap and rework.) This in turn, improved productivity and throughput, as well as freeing up capacity for increased production.

This was all achieved without additional investment in the plant or equipment. Each step contributed to the next and to the bottom-line. The value of improved customer satisfaction and company reputation for quality which are difficult to calculate will result in increased sales revenues.

Continuing Gains: As new skills generated cascading gains, and were incorporated into the hiring and supervisory process, they also promote the continuation of the new practices. Some argue that such gains continue forever, but that is not always true. Often, people involved make improvements, solve their immediate problems, and become comfortable with the new levels of activity, they forget what they have learned. Keeping learning fresh on a consistent basis helps promote steady, continuing gains. Know that when opportunities surge again, the organization is set to reap the rewards.

Spontaneous Discoveries: In the process of facilitating training, the facilitator and the participants may make valuable spontaneous discoveries of great potential gains. Often, these are totally above and beyond anything in the course content. The challenge is to recognize and capture these discoveries.

These "aha" moments are often lost when the person who has the responsibility to communicate this valuable information or who should be informed is not involved. In situations where the Unit Leader is involved the problem is avoided because they have the authority and leverage to seize these opportunities. Throughout this book, you'll see several examples of how these "aha" moments are captured and move the organization forward in a new and profitable way.

Forever Gains: It is easy to forget ideas, methods and information learned in the training session. Yet the ones that are retained and used successfully reap rewards forever. This is a continuing, legacy of gains from training once provided, and a great facilitator is able to link the individuals to this type of learning and reinforce it for future reference.

Propagation: Gains achieved in one location are sometimes reproducible in others and the potential gains are multiplied. When setting up training sessions explore how the potential gains could be propagated to other areas.

Application of These Ideas

The most significant ideas in this chapter for me were:

_____

As a result I intend to:

_____

Action Prompt:

- Enter your intended action(s) in your daily planner or computer scheduler.

Resources Available:

- The Unique Six Step Job Instruction Form that Pete said was his greatest gain is available free at FusionOrFizzle.com
- The Unique Cost/Benefit Analysis Form can be downloaded for free at FusionorFizzle.com. (Be sure to check with your finance department first to determine if such a form already exists in your organization—if so, use that as it adds credibility and avoids duplication.)

Section II

The Seven Best Practices for Training Excellence and Maximum Impact

Over many years, in a wide variety of organizations we have seen the vast differences achieved from various leadership and management training efforts. While great gains are achieved by some, others realize lesser gains. In a few cases, training poorly done and lack of interest by management combine to create negative reactions and disappointment for all.

Through these decades of experience we have discovered that relatively few factors determine the success or failure—the *fusion* or *fizzle* that the organization achieves. Therefore, each is vitally important. We've developed a list of seven best practices for maximizing the results. Following this process generally leads to:

- Greater training effectiveness
- Added value to participants
- Improved retention of knowledge and skills
- Significant contribution to organizational goals
- Continued application and sustainability of the gains

The Seven Best Practices in the following chapters include many real life examples and success stories from small, mid-size and large companies. The variety of organizations and their products and services indicates the broad applicability of these practices.

The Seven Best Practices

- 1 -

Empower a Leadership Development Team to
maximize leverage, synergy, support and sustainability.

- 2 -

Scrutinize all needs and opportunities, then
prioritize plans and resources based on potential impact on results.

- 3 -

Select a trainer/facilitator with the skills and methods
best able to achieve the predetermined goals and outcomes.

- 4 -

Crystallize, focus and communicate the
expectations.

- 5 -

Launch training initiatives with dynamic leadership then
monitor progress and take positive action to ensure success.

- 6 -

Celebrate enthusiastically and affirm achievements,
then record and report the gains.

- 7 -

Refine and repeat the process to achieve
competitive advantage, sustainability and culture change.

Chapter 3

Best Practice One

Empower a Leadership Development Team to Maximize Leverage

It generates common purpose, ensures focus, and merges the leader's leverage with the synergism of the team.

Leadership and learning are indispensable to each other.

–*John F. Kennedy*

INSPIRE

Best Practice One

Empower a Leadership Development Team to maximize leverage, synergy, support and sustainability.

Training is the process of providing instructions and developing skills, which enable a person to actually perform a task or a function. The success of training therefore can be measured by whether behaviors have changed for the better. It is creating "know how" and "can do." The "will do" factor however, is dependent on authority, opportunity and motivation. Unfortunately the word "training" is a broad, all-encompassing term often used equally for job instruction training all the way to people skills and on occasion to corporate strategy formulation.

Education on the other hand is the presentation of information about past events, concepts, practices and research results. It is often theoretical and is intended to increase the knowledge base and conceptual understanding of the recipient for possible future application of that knowledge to similar and non-similar situations.

Training as we define it above, is only a portion of a larger more complex challenge called development. Development goes beyond training and includes such elements as job rotation, special assignments and projects and/or coaching and mentoring by the "boss" or others.

We suggest that both training and development should be directed by a Leadership Development Team (LDT) of three to five senior managers including the organization's Unit Leader, the HR person and one or more of the operations people. The reason is that this will ensure that a wide spectrum of organizational and individual needs are identified, mutually agreed upon priorities are established, effective training is delivered and the learned skills applied. Using such a team also generates greater support and oversight for the efforts and ensures the predetermined results and outcomes are actually achieved. It also fosters sustainability.

Do You Understand Our Vision?

The CEO of one of the largest healthcare facilities on the west coast who uses these principles in managing his staff reported that when he has a performance situation with a senior manager, he begins by asking, "Do you understand our vision?"

If the answer is yes he asks, "Do you know how and can you do what's required to make that happen or do you require additional training?" This CEO said that sometimes the person admits to needing training, sometimes they simply want a decision made for them. If they say they don't need training, he suggests that they go and do what needs to be done. This process tells him whether that individual is a leader, a leaner, or a processor:

Leaders take the initiative to make things happen.

Leaners want others to do what they are capable of doing themselves.

Processors are those who keep busy doing repetitive, routine, sometimes non-essential activities.

This latter group goes through the motions, following a familiar routine, attending meetings and processing paperwork but that is the limit of their contribution. They feel safe and comfortable in this self-created undemanding niche. This CEO stresses his commitment to putting "care" into healthcare and asks them to do the same. This value is his primary guide in day-to-day operations and meetings.

Leadership, Vision, Values, Mission and Goals

A true leader has a vision of the organization as it must become, and articulates the values of the organization that guide it in its day-to-day decisions and behaviors. The leader also focuses on the mission and on major objectives to be achieved.

Even more important, the leader regularly connects these elements to the agenda topics being discussed in meetings. Therefore, everyone knows they are his or her priorities, guiding principles, beliefs and operating philosophy. They know as well, that these are more than just words on a banner, poster or plaque.

Finally, these dynamic organizational leaders realize that goals and strategies are only achievable when their managers, supervisors and employees have the knowledge and skills—the ability to "make it happen" and "to get it done."

The Leader's Balancing Act: Task versus People Focus

Some organizations are overly *task focused*. In this kind of workplace, only measurable results are considered important. This singular focus, over time creates a feeling that no person is significant; that only the numbers matter. Employees and their managers come to believe the organization doesn't value them in any way. They are expendable. With this all-pervasive climate, morale declines, employee turnover increases, and key performance results begin to decline. Resulting in just the opposite condition that management's initial focus was intended to achieve. And making the situation worse, management often becomes even more emphatic that results need to improve, compounding the problem.

Other organizations are overly *people focused*. The culture tends to become bureaucratic and unresponsive to customer/client needs. Endless meetings, and deferred decisions are used as attempts to generate buy-in and inclusion. The attempt to make everyone happy by asking little of them actually results in dissatisfaction, lower morale and unhappiness. Once again, just the opposite from what was intended and needed. The goal is having both a task focus and a people focus. Doing both well is the most engaging and highest performing culture. The leader has the challenge of promoting both accountability for results and encouragement to grow in capability and performance.

> **Therefore, this first best practice focuses on empowering a Leadership Development Team. Its purpose is to develop the leaders within the group, maximize their inherent synergy, support them in their tasks and create a sustainable and productive environment.**

The leaders must formulate, and inculcate the operating principles in the organization. They must demonstrate by word and example that they support these principles and lead by example. Their personal productivity and conduct as managers is a vital guidepost to others. Managers, supervisors and team leaders must communicate regularly, demonstrating their personal commitment to the values and principles.

Some years ago an article in *Fortune* magazine said, "That a company's operating principles seem to be an individual version of the Boy Scout Law: the main principles are excellence of quality, reliability of performance and loyalty in relationships." These could be termed motherhood and apple pie but they become more than that once they are put into practice.

Two of our sons worked for McDonalds during high school and still remember the three principals they were trained to follow which were, "Quality, service and cleanliness." When employees see that management takes these seriously, a genuine pride develops in their work, in the product and in the company.

The Details: Through establishing a Leadership Development Team (LDT), you are creating a powerful force that will positively impact your financial bottom-line and working environment—from top to bottom within the organization. This process involves bringing together supervisors, Unit Leaders, line managers, human resource professionals, finance people and an external trainer/facilitator team in the ongoing leadership development process. Here are some of their key functions and responsibilities:

1. First, this group develops a clear definition of what constitutes effective leadership behavior in their organization.

2. The team is made accountable for the selection of the trainer/ facilitator. They are responsible for the implementation, application of the skills, and determining the contribution to organizational goals and achievement of sustainability.

3. The team considers the organization's strategic initiatives for competitiveness and growth, planned changes, problem-opportunities and the developmental plans for individuals. Then it prepares a brief situational summary and a list of training needs based on information gathered as suggested in Best Practice Two.

4. The team is lead by a common understanding, focus and unity. Every member of the team is responsible for being enthusiastic and positive. They must act as examples to others and display the behaviors they expect others to adopt. In summary, members need to be cheerleaders rather than critics. This is vital, because criticism, no matter how well intended, delivered, or deserved, will foster a natural tendency to cover, distort, deny or minimize problems—

thereby foiling the elimination of those problems and the gains that could accrue.

5. They identify and prioritize training and development needs. The benefit is that a broader range of viewpoints are considered. Everyone has an opportunity—in fact a responsibility—to contribute to the assessment and purpose of the team. It gives them, individually, the feeling that they have had their say and creates buy-in. When the final decisions are made, they understand the basis for those decisions. The decisions are better and the support for the implementation is stronger.

6. They determine the training for lead hands, team leaders, supervisors and managers and secondary specialized training for specific employees based on their needs. They also consider their own needs in their specific roles.

7. Training is directly aligned with the outcome expected. The LDT clearly defines the expected gains.

8. The team assigns a coach/expediter/mentor to assist participants in applying the methods, achieving results and recording them. The coach/mentor will have experience, patience, and a natural inclination towards mentoring should relish the opportunity. In smaller organizations, the coach or mentor may be a member of the LDT.

9. After a person learns the skills taught through the training, reinforcement and application is required. This can include follow-up coaching and direction after the learning is complete to ensure application and demonstrated capability. The changed behaviors should be documented and shared by the participants along with an observation about the impact on his or her department.

10. Members must recognize that there may be a time when no one knows how to do what needs to be done. It is normal and natural that at times one or more of the team will lack the required knowledge and ability. In either of these

situations the Unit Leader with the help of HR must conduct a search for the necessary external expertise. Once located and engaged, this individual or group must be considered a member of the team and their role defined, expectations communicated, information shared. They must understand that their responsibilities cannot be delegated. Team members continue to be responsible for achieving the goals and supporting the efforts of the external "expert."

The Benefits for the Key Members

People are motivated when they have "buy-in." Without it, they lose focus, commitment and perseverance. To promote "buy-in," it is essential they know how they will benefit through their participation:

The Unit Leader:

- Gains input from these key people, and their unique background and experience.

- Has an opportunity to share the organizational strategies, goals, and priorities.

- Utilizes the power of synergy to generate support.

- Has a conduit for reinforcing his or her vision, values, beliefs and common purpose.

- Gains a deeper understanding of the skills and strengths of the team members and their developmental needs.

The HR Manager:

- Has an opportunity to share the HR perspective on issues, particularly behavioral issues.

- Gains a better understanding of the Unit Leader's and managers beliefs, concerns and priorities.

- Can suggest actions and policies that will produce the best results. A key responsibility for the HR person is to link behaviors to performance. Others on the team may be inclined to focus only on measurable results and the natural tendency of HR people is inclined towards observable behaviors.

- Increases the probability of success by involving leaders with operational responsibility who ultimately supervise the work of the people being trained.

The Operational Manager(s):

- Gains understanding of the organization's strategies and priorities.

- Develops a better understanding of the HR experience and behavioral viewpoint.

- Has an opportunity to raise operational issues, needs and add suggestions.

The Finance Representative:

- Hears the concerns and challenges of the managers and their viewpoint on what they need other than the usual tools, supplies and equipment and how this will impact their numbers.

- Achieves a better understanding to the budget needs of the HR department and how these are expected to contribute to achieving better bottom-line results.

The responsibility of the Finance person is unique and four-fold:

- **First**, to assist in evaluating potential initiatives for prioritizing.

- **Second,** to suggest other initiatives that could be valuable and worthwhile.

- **Third,** to provide relevant information to participants.

- **Fourth,** to record and report the gains to the LDT.

- For this task, select a person who not only has a broad knowledge of the organization, and its operating costs but also is positive and helpful.

- Their responsibility is not to minimize or undermine the extent of the gains but to encourage participants and offer useful suggestions for expanding and presenting their gains.

- This person also needs to understand that behavior change and changed methods are necessary to achieve measurable results.

The Trainer/Facilitator (whether internal or an external resource):

- Gains understanding of the perspectives and priorities of other members.

- Has an opportunity to share insights gained while conducting previous training sessions.

- Can identify hindrances to performance that participants may have shared.

- Has the opportunity to report spontaneous discoveries emanating from participants.

Synergy and the Team

Once the LDT is capable, clear and committed to following the vision, values, and mission, there is a powerful, magnetic force that exists. Synergy has been explained as $2 + 2 = 5$. The sum is greater than the total of its individual parts. When team members are in synch, sparks fly, there is *fusion*, excitement and enthusiasm. There is trust, confidence, and energy.

One aspect a Unit Leader must avoid is using a team of those who always agree with him or her and never raise issues. This is like operating with blinders that limit the field of vision and blocks potentially better ideas and methods. Dissenting opinions may be correct. Even if they are not, there may be issues that deserve more discussion and preparation. Once a decision has been finalized the total team is expected to support it.

Leadership Practices Applicable to Larger Entities

From a large company perspective, we might have expected failure in the situations we described earlier; after all only one company had an HR specialist. None had an in-house trainer. Most of the key people had only a minimum education; there were no MBAs in any of the firms. Their reporting systems were basic. However, what they had was commitment to succeed and a willingness to apply new methods.

These small businesses were successful, primarily, because the owner was a leader and this was demonstrated by the fact that he knew he had problems and admitted that he didn't have solutions, nor did any of his team. They all knew the problems existed without looking at a stack of reports or their computer screens. They saw the actual scrap being discarded and the pieces waiting to be reworked or repaired. They had never heard of MBWA (Management by Walking Around.) It was what they did as a normal part of their duties. When they walked around they knew what to look for—where to look –and who to talk with about what was happening—and they knew what it was costing the company. What they didn't know was how to fix what was happening. They didn't know what the "better way" was but they:

- Were willing to reach outside the company for assistance and expertise.

- Participated in all of the sessions.

- Began to implement the improvements the next day. (Action oriented rather than discussion obsessed.)

- Didn't point fingers at others; they accepted responsibility for both what was happening and for making changes.

- Supported each other in implementing the new methods.

- Knew when new methods were effective because they saw the results for themselves.

These elements invariably produced measurable results, rapid payback, high ROI and significant improvement to the bottom-line. Plus, working together improved co-operation, teamwork, mutual respect, and possibly most important—a sense of self-confidence and a sense of achievement and empowerment. They felt un-stoppable. Euphoric!

In Chapter Two, the example titled *At Remark Electric*, was a corporate business unit rather than a small business. In this case, the problem was solved because three key management people collaborated.

The plant manager didn't attend the sessions, but discussed his concerns frankly with the HR specialist and decided on the action they would take—together. Again, they accessed an external training resource. Equally, and possibly most important, they discussed their concerns and proposed a solution with the person being trained and agreed on the purpose and desired outcomes of the training. Here we see positive leverage at its finest. Not threats or coercion but coaching and assistance—an avenue for improved skills—a path that allows the individual to maintain self-esteem. At the same time the company and its management developed a person who obviously has potential and will be a more valuable asset in future. Everyone in this scenario wins, and so they should!

Ovation Automotive: Successes and Deficiencies

The progressive, serialized story and experience of this company will appear with each of the Seven Best Practices found in this book. You'll learn more about their successes and deficiencies as they develop a training capability and launch their first management/leadership course.

The New Leader Faces a Deteriorating Disaster: Ovation Automotive Inc. had twenty-six plants worldwide with five located in one region. Tom Garrison was recently appointed president of Canadian operations. Tom came with significant experience from their Kentucky and Tennessee USA plants where he had previously been plant manager of their largest plant in that area.

This assignment was both an opportunity to gain experience with broader responsibilities and to determine his ability to turn around a group of plants where performance had been declining for almost three years. The potential rewards would likely be promotion to a region in Europe and eventually to corporate headquarters in New York.

With a tour of the five plants accomplished, his initial week of meetings with his management concluded and an analysis of operating reports completed, Tom knew there was a formidable list of actions necessary.

The Situation at Ovation Automation Inc.: Tom was appalled at the condition of the facilities, which had been allowed to deteriorate in an effort to control costs. Scrap at the largest of the plants was usually in the *daily* range of $50,000 to $100,000 and created a horrendous financial drain and a bottleneck to productivity. Employee grievances were so numerous that they were overwhelming the labor relations manager and his assistant. Many of these issues were due to the actions and behaviors of the supervisors.

Everyone was busy firefighting, trying to cope with what appeared to be impossible problems. Managers and supervisors seemed unable to stabilize or improve the situation. Realizing that he had to take action on several fronts concurrently and quickly, Tom first prioritized the operational problems. Then he began to implement preventive measures and tackle root causes such as developing the ability of the supervisors and managers. (At that time, Tom was unaware of the Seven Best Practices but he knew intuitively much of what had to be done.)

The Solution: Tom realized that his management team had to stem the flow of new and repeat problems. "We have to stop the bleeding—and switch to a problem prevention mode," he said. Similarly, he knew that this was not a "lack-of-motivation situation," but a lack of supervisory and management "know-how" condition. Quickly, he assembled a team to formulate the plans and begin to implement them. He appointed one of his key managers George Whitney, Manager of Continuous Improvement tasking him with prioritizing the problem-opportunities. Next a manager of training and development, Tony Apostle, was recruited and challenged to find a supervisory leadership training program with terminology, methods and practices which were appropriate. And at the same time, ensure the facilitator(s) knew manufacturing situations, and could deliver the training and make it relevant and interesting.

Tom's team, as they became known, now consisted of George (Manager of Continuous Improvement), Tony (Training & Development Manager), Bill Kelly (one of the most dynamic and progressive plant managers) and of course Tom himself. Tom reminded them on a regular basis, "We are going to make our plants the best in the corporation—and we need supervisors and managers who can see this vision and make it happen."

Ovation's Progress Report

(Progress is rated in terms of Grim, Good, Great or To Be Determined)

Great: Tom was a leader *in action*, and a bold leader by example:

- He formed a team and tasked each person with relevant responsibilities.

- Two new positions were created and staffed providing the resources and the focus necessary to speed action.

- Wisely, he tackled both immediate operational problems and the deeper issue of supervisory and managerial capability—realizing they were related and vital.

To Be Determined: At this point, there was no plan to directly link the skills developed to specific application and results. The issue of coaching and sustainability were not considered and would prove to be a stumbling block in future as we will see.

Finally: A commendable beginning. Tom intuitively did much of what is suggested in Best Practice One. He created and empowered a Leadership Development Team and remained personally involved, contributing a sense of urgency and rapid action.

Application of the Ideas in this Chapter

The most significant ideas in this chapter for me were:

_____

_____

_____

As a result, I intend to:

_____

_____

_____

Action Prompt

- Identify which managers, if any, *now* participate in the planning process for leadership/management training and enter their names here:

- Which managers *should be* part of your Leadership Development Team, either on a continuing or rotating basis to make the planning more relevant and effective?

- Enter your intended action (s) in your daily planner.
- When would be the most favorable time to do this?

- What first step you could take now?

    In the next chapter, discover the vast potential for gains in organizations, including how to identify them and prioritize the pursuit of those gains.

Chapter 4

Best Practice Two

Scrutinize All Needs and Opportunities Based on Potential Results

Reason: To allocate limited resources to the areas of greatest potential gains and do it with the input and commitment of the team.

INSPIRE

There are no such things as limits to growth,
because there are no limits to the human capacity
for intelligence, imagination, and wonder.

–Ronald Regan

Best Practice Two

Scrutinize all needs and opportunities, then
prioritize plans and resources based
on potential impact on results.

This process is very focused and responsive to needs. The solution—determining the training needs and implementation plans—is directly linked to the information derived. Now, let's put this team to work…

The Details: Have the Leadership Development Team consider all anticipated changes, problem-opportunities, and competitive challenges, then prioritize training plans on the basis of expected impact on outcomes to achieving organizational strategies, competitive advantage and payback. This will focus the limited resources available on the greatest payback opportunities.

Ensure sufficient funding for training excellence, personal coaching for individuals who request it, follow-up reinforcement and application sessions. Do it all to ensure skills are developed and applied successfully.

The Benefits: All members have input, and develop understanding of organizational priorities. This avoids the many disappointments, misunderstandings and frustrations so often prevalent. Key members of the LDT benefit as follows:

The Unit Leader:

- Knows that input from the LDT ensures that all needs and potential gains have been considered and the reasons for each manager's recommendations.

- Gains a wider perspective of what others consider to be the needs and potential opportunities. At the same time others hear the leader's viewpoint and opinions.

- Quickly gains an estimation of how much potential is likely to be realized and the reliability of the information team members identify.

- Has a more complete and factual basis on which to make budgetary decisions.

The HR Leader:

- Has a channel for proposing appropriate training solutions for problems and for longer-range developmental initiatives.

- Can anticipate greater support for both requests and the actual initiatives.

The Line Manager:

- Has an opportunity to request needed training support and the reasons.

- Understands how training initiatives can contribute to solving operational issues.

- Knows areas where he/she will be expected to ensure application, results and sustainability.

The Trainer/Facilitator:

- Can contribute input regarding process and systemic issues which are restricting performance and where training could result in improvements.

- Better understands the perceived needs and priorities of the organization.

- Has clarity as to the expectations of the organization and can recommend personal action by the managers regarding coaching and mentoring support required.

Are Your People Ready?

"Your people are your company's most important asset," reads the first line in a recent advertisement in leading business publications. CEO's have made similar statements for decades. Do they believe it? Do they demonstrate it? Are leaders at all levels demonstrating it?

The advertisement continues with, "They (the employees) come to work each day full of ambition, ideas, plans and goals. How do you harness this energy? How do you make it work for you?" Questions we would suggest are:

- Are your employees ready? Are the management team, HR and the Unit Leader ready and able?

- Are they ready to be the competitive advantage your organization needs?

- Will they be more effective and more efficient in the year ahead?

- Will they be more competent and more committed?

- Are they preparing for upcoming challenges and opportunities?

Another recent advertisement captures our beliefs succinctly, it reads:

**Opportunity...it's everywhere when
you know where to look.**

**Creating, seizing and igniting
opportunity is what it's all about.**

–Bank of America Advertisement

An Opportunity-Problem Arises

Al Bartolli, President of Niagara Tubing Corp. could be called "A president's president." His Italian heritage provided a permanent healthy tanned appearance. His black hair was combed straight back with not a hair out of place. A navy blue suit with a barely perceptible pin-stripe, white shirt and striped tie reflected the ultimate in corporate image. Only one word could adequately describe his appearance and that is, "impeccable." His desk was devoid of all clutter except for one letter. The impression was one of stark efficiency and effectiveness. It said, "Get to the point I'm busy."

Fortunately, during the exchange of pleasantries at our first meeting we discovered a degree of commonality. We had both been employed by the same corporation, in the same city although in different functions and at different times. These similarities quickly generated a friendly rapport. Al shared the fact that while with the corporation, as a plant manager, a recruiter had called with an irresistible offer. Al accepted and became president of this firm, Niagara Tubing Corp., a manufacturer of architectural and automotive steel tubing and part of an integrated conglomerate.

The Situation at Niagara Tubing Corp.: While we chatted, it seemed that Al's attention was elsewhere. A small frown remained in place and seemed unrelated to our discussion. On impulse I asked, "Al I can't help but notice your frown, do you mind if I ask what's causing you concern?" He seemed to welcome the opportunity to vent his restrained emotions.

"Frankly, I'm frustrated," he began, "one of our customers is offering us more of their business. We now get about half and a competitor gets the balance. For the past year the customer has been having difficulty on their assembly line in fitting the pieces we supply with those of our competitor. Each of us blames the other for the slight differences in tolerances. Unfortunately the customer then has to arbitrate the disputes. Their proposed solution is to purchase both pieces from us."

"So why the frown?" I asked again. "You should be celebrating the added volume to your top line."

Al responded, "It's because my people are saying that we can't handle it. They claim we don't have the capacity."

Now it was my turn, "Well if you can't, obviously you can't, why the frown?"

With the frustration now more obvious he exploded, "Because my gut tells me that we should be able to do this!"

The Solution: "Sounds like a project for Value Analysis," I suggested. It was obvious that he was speechless. (Al had witnessed the power of Value Analysis (VA) earlier in his career and was disappointed he hadn't thought of it himself.) In that instant he realized that VA was exactly the process appropriate for this situation.

"Do you people do Value Analysis?" he asked incredulously.

"We have an associate who has both the credentials and experience," was the reply.

In an instant, his question was, "How soon can you provide me with a proposal?"

Our question was, "How quickly do you need it?"

"I need it for a meeting at two o'clock this afternoon," he said emphatically.

"Direct me to an office with a computer and you will have it before lunch. That will give you time to review it before the meeting."

The frown was gone; in its place was a triumphant "Aha" smile. As promised the proposal was completed. At four o'clock that afternoon Al called to say that the proposal was accepted and invited us to return the next day to finalize the details.

Two teams were rapidly formed and the results were beyond what was expected. The details follow, but first, a summary of what Value Analysis is for those unfamiliar with the process.

What is Value Analysis?

Value Analysis was first formulated by a senior procurement manager at General Electric some six decades ago as a structured process to examine the function of products, services and systems to identify alternate ways of achieving the same function at a lower cost without sacrificing quality or on-time delivery to the customer. It has evolved over many years since, and there have been many adaptations for a wide range of applications. It may now be referred to as Value Management, Value Engineering, Functional Analysis, Activity Value Analysis, Design for Manufacture and numerous other titles.

Teams generally receive three to five days of training, which covers such topics as functional analysis, development of a F.A.S.T. Diagram (Functional Analysis System Technique,) brainstorming, idea evaluation, prioritizing solutions and "selling" solutions to senior management. It concludes with monitoring implementation and reporting progress to ensure successful conclusion.

The Results: The teams found that by moving two bottleneck operations to a parallel concurrent position, they were able to achieve major gains in throughput:

- In doing so the company was able to accept the additional business with minimum investment or disruption.

- Plus, while gathering information in the initial phase, the team learned that scrap on this production line was running at 18%. Since this was stainless steel, it was very costly.

- Further they discovered that the tubing, during the forming stages, was being picked up and put down six times. Often during these moves the tubing was damaged and this was the chief cause of the high scrap rate.

- In brainstorming the teams were able to reduce the number of transfers to only three, which reduced damage and scrap and at the same time further improved throughput.

- To gain additional ideas, the teams invited a senior representative from the customer's company to review the FAST diagram and comment. In just a few minutes, the guest said, "I see here that you spray your tubing with an anti-rust solution before shipping. That's not necessary," he continued, "because we are a just-in-time operation and the tubing is used within two days of receipt. Further," he continued, "I notice that you cut the tubing to a standard length before shipment. That is unnecessary as well, because we cut it several times in our production process, so random lengths are not a problem and in fact could be an advantage."

- Eliminating these operations generated savings that were shared by both parties. It was truly a win-win situation. Needless to say Al was in a state of high satisfaction.

- Niagara obtained the additional business, which increased top line revenue.

- Product cost was lowered because of reduced scrap and improved throughput.

- The realignment of two operations further increased throughput.

- The gains went directly to the bottom-line.

- The customer was pleased as well, solidifying the customer-supplier relationship.

- Let's not forget the team members. They gained important new skills, contributed to a significant project, received their certificate of participation presented in the president's office and followed by lunch with the president who thanked each one personally.

Follow-up—A Necessary Element

This story is not over. Shortly after this success Al called again with several new projects, which also were successful. However, an internal political situation now developed. The manager of industrial engineering approached Al saying that he was certain that he could lead the next project which was to be a major effort and thereby save the fees paid to our firm as an external consultant. Al called to apologize but said he had to give his manager this opportunity to prove himself, which was understandable.

Three months later Al called again, this time asking if we would take over the two teams that their manager had established. Not only were they not making progress but conflict and bickering were straining relationships and eroding co-operation. It seems the manager had constituted teams that were too large and unwieldy, and had selected members on the basis of favoritism. In addition, team members complained that the manager paid scant attention to their ideas and instead was pressuring them to implement ideas that he had already formulated.

This highlights the fact that in many situations, external resources have the required expertise honed by years of experience in a wide variety of challenges. While internal people have important capabilities and knowledge, they simply have not had the opportunity to gain the same degree of expertise.

> External resources, because they are independent
> of the organization are often perceived as more
> objective. Therefore participants generally work
> together more openly without hidden agendas.
> For much the same reason, participants often
> share their concerns, observations and suggestions
> more openly with an external resource person.

Observations: Training people and HR people will gain greater support from senior management when they link their proposals and requests to achievement of the organization's goals. In doing this, they gain credibility and support. At the same time, it is vital that they do not claim to be proficient in all areas. Doing so and subsequently failing erodes the very credibility they require from their leaders.

Assessing Potential Maximizes Results: Identifying potential before setting a goal often results in a higher goal and greater results because those involved realize the extent of the potential.

Valuable leadership training and experience can often be gained through involvement in non-profit civic organizations. Leading such committees with specific projects in a risk-free situation develops skills and learning beyond what may be available in one's current career situation.

Participating in the annual United Way campaigns and in-company campaigns, and later in the citywide campaigns and on their local board of directors was an unforgettable learning experience. Most impressive was the organization's ability to recruit and train hundreds of volunteers for each year's campaign. Then a year later they repeat the process. In contrast, other organizations tend to use the same devoted volunteers year after year until they become "burned out" and leave; their talents lost forever. Also, these organizations often use the same methods and practices long after they have lost their relevance and effectiveness.

The reason for including this example is because of a campaign strategy which The United Way introduced, which could be useful to our readers. This seemingly minor change caused a major shift in both campaigner strategy and contributor thinking when establishing goals for giving.

Traditionally, key volunteers who assisted organizations in preparing for their in-company campaigns set the goals for the upcoming campaign based on the past year's actual results. They look at last year's results, decide on the desired increase and communicate that as a target. What other approach was there? Well, the United Way named it "Campaigning to Potential."

At the first stage of the effort, the previous year's numbers were considered but only to determine the "unachieved potential." It began by reviewing the percentage of employees who contributed. Which usually ranged somewhere between 60 to 95%. Therefore, the first goal was to increase the percentage of *givers* to a figure closer to potential.

Next, actual *donor givings* were analyzed and the amount being contributed by *the top 10%* was calculated. Once done, the number of potential donors was multiplied by the average of the top 10%. This always produced a surprising number. This number, the average of the top 10% was suggested as a number to be communicated to all potential donors for their consideration. Finally, a lower number was also developed and communicated. It was what the *average* donor gave and it was also multiplied by the total number of potential donors.

What does this not-for-profit example have to do with leadership development? The answer is everything! When we consider the performance of our organizations in terms of potential—that is in comparison with the best division—the best plant—the best department or our most successful competitor—then we begin thinking in terms of what is truly possible. In many cases this is what is necessary to achieve market leadership, competitive advantage and work class status.

The United Way also uses what it terms, "Leaders-of-the-Way" to set the example for donations. These companies conduct their in-plant campaigns several weeks earlier than the community-wide campaign. Their results are then communicated through the news media. Doing this provides recognition for those companies and their employees for what they have achieved. However, the greater purpose is to demonstrate to other employee groups what has been done, providing a target for which to strive.

This "potential" thinking is vital to achieving "Best in Class" or "Industry Leader" designations. It becomes the catalyst for focusing the organization's efforts. It motivates. It creates synergism, with everyone striving together toward a common target.

Consider Problems as Indicators of Training Needs

Through research conducted while writing our previous book, *Employees Not Doing What You Expect* it became apparent that a relatively few elements cause the vast majority of problems. **The number one reason was change.** When change occurs or is introduced, difficulties and problems become evident. In normal operations employees and managers cope with minor day-to-day difficulties with relative ease. But major changes throw many off balance and they feel unprepared, threatened and inadequate.

These changes may be in the areas of technology, competition, legislation, products, markets, suppliers, the economy, and significant variations in volumes both increases and decreases.

In some cases, the reasons are insufficient planning, inadequate resources or a lack of training. An associate expressed what happens this way: "When budgets are being prepared, management approves the projected costs for buildings, equipment, supplies, computer hardware and software but when they arrive at funds for employee communications and training, they arbitrarily make reductions that impair effective delivery. They under-fund these *people* needs and wonder why they are having problems." She continued, "Management wouldn't think of only roofing one half of a building or eliminating the painting inside or insisting employees make do with only half of the equipment, tools or supplies, yet they do this to the training allocation."

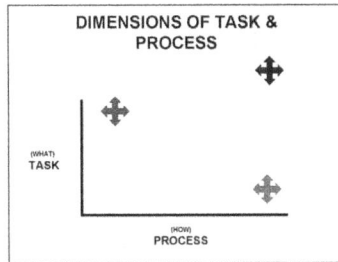

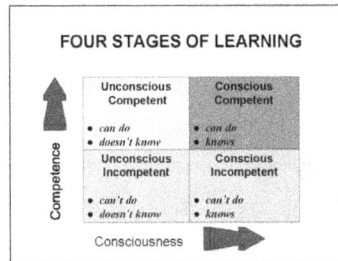

DIMENSIONS OF TASK & PROCESS

(WHAT) **TASK**

(HOW) **PROCESS**

FOUR STAGES OF LEARNING

	Unconscious Competent	Conscious Competent
	• *can do* • *doesn't know*	• *can do* • *knows*
Competence	Unconscious Incompetent	Conscious Incompetent
	• *can't do* • *doesn't know*	• *can't do* • *knows*

Consciousness

Training Needs–Opportunities and Unrealized Potential

Traditionally, HR and training people use a number of techniques for identifying training needs. Among them are questionnaires, surveys, interviews and focus meetings. Each is valid and useful to an extent. One of the models that we find helpful in considering needs is shown next.

Noel Burch from Gordon Training International originally developed the Four Stages of Learning any New Skill model. It has since been adopted as the Four Stages of Learning.

**The goal is to have everyone become
Conscious Competent.**

It means they are capable, realize it and are therefore, confident in carrying out their duties. The most serious situations are those who are Unconscious Incompetent.

Unconscious Incompetents do not realize a need for training and therefore they struggle to identify their own training needs. If their supervisor or manager fails to identify the need, performance suffers. It is an important requirement that leaders understand and communicate these training needs.

The Conscious Incompetents usually respond to training opportunities to correct their known needs. These are usually referred to as felt needs.

Those who are Unconscious Competents fortunately are capable and doing the job well but may be hesitant because they do not understand the extent of their true abilities and may be reluctant to accept greater responsibility. These people can also struggle with change because their success is driven by habits and changing those habits requires conscious reflection.

Similarly, the HR and training people may have difficulty in identifying these needs. Sometimes it is because of their position in the company. They may not be included in the organization's planning and goal setting meetings. Therefore they are unaware of the organization's goals and cannot connect their budget requests to the organization's needs.

As a result, they have difficulty in convincing management of budget needs. **Neither party connects what they need and are attempting to accomplish with those of the other party.** The result is frustration, unfulfilled gaps and shortfalls, which tend to erode credibility and confidence.

The Solution: All parties need to understand the ultimate purpose of training and its expected contribution to the organization's goals:

- The value and extent of unrealized potential.

- The organization's upcoming changes and challenges that are opportunities.

The Training Needs Identification

When considering training needs, the Leadership Development Team (LDT) should start at the top. This means beginning with the Unit Leader, regardless of that person's title.

- What are the developmental needs of the Unit Leader? What knowledge and skills would contribute to this person's success?

- Does this person, know how to develop a vision, values and beliefs statement to guide the organization?

- Can he/she identify and communicate the three to six most important goals to be achieved and do this on a regular basis?

- Is he/she an effective communicator and able to present the vision, values, and the goals to the employees and managers?

- Can the person conduct positive, productive performance reviews and can she/he address performance and behavioral deficiencies?

- Can this Unit Leader lead productive meetings?

- Does this person have the persuasion, negotiating, coaching, and other leadership skills needed to be more effective and to prepare them for increased responsibility?

Typical Training and Educational Experiences of Leaders

- Through our extensive experience, we've heard it all in regards to the types of training leaders do—and do not—receive. The following is not intended as an all-encompassing list. Use it to help consider potential experiences when assessing leaders needs for training:

- The newly appointed CEO of an internationally known mining corporation told a business reporter, "I've been training myself my entire career for this appointment."

- The authors of *In Search of Excellence* noted, "None of the men we studied, relied on personal magnetism. All *made* themselves into effective leaders."

- While working with a client company, the vice president of manufacturing shared the fact that several years prior he had enrolled in a sales course. "I felt I needed the sales skills to be more persuasive with my supervisors, employees and union people and oh yes, with the president."

- A chief engineer with a staff of almost 60 people when asked regarding skills he felt he most needed said, "I avoid holding meetings with my direct reports as a group because I simply can't deal with the banter and conflicts."

- The dean of a prominent business school told an interviewer that he usually enrolls in one course each year saying, "It's the only way I can keep up with the changing business world."

> **Unit Leaders increasingly are utilizing external facilitators to act as their personal coaches. Whether the title is Personal Coach, Executive Coach, or Business Coach, they serve as capable and trusted sounding boards for leaders who feel isolated and welcome impartial advice, fresh ideas and confidential coaching.**

This trend is likely to continue and extend to all of those at the management and executive levels. The value they add is their interpersonal skills, business acumen, management experience and ability to hold frank non-threatening discussions on a one-on-one basis. HR and the LDT would do well to identify one or more such qualified people to act as advisors or coaches on an as needed basis.

Front line leaders can also benefit from having access to individual coaching assistance if requested. In some cases they may have a question or issue that they have been unwilling to raise during the training session. This may be something that has troubled them for some time and can finally be resolved with coaching.

HR Has Developmental Needs As Well

HR people deserve great empathy and support. They are the recipients of most if not all problems—and are sometimes asked to shoulder the blame. If on the other hand all is going well, employees and managers are being productive; the credit usually goes to the individual manager rather than to the HR people.

Add to this, the broad spectrum of responsibilities the HR department carries. There may include compensation and benefit administration, salaried employee policies and procedures, labor relations and contract negotiation, health and safety, recruiting and interviewing, human resources training and development, employee and manager counseling, human resource planning, succession planning, the performance evaluation system and the recognition and reward process. Too often, HR is expected to have expertise in all of these areas—and personally conduct any training programs themselves.

Making the job more challenging, HR might be excluded from executive meetings or if invited are treated as if they are second-tier participants with little input or influence. HR needs to be updated on emerging government legislation and the latest strategies for employee recruiting and retention and the specialized courses available in each one of their responsibility areas. They also need skills in negotiating, counseling, questioning, listening and persuading.

> TIP: In his best seller *Winning*, Jack Welch says, "Elevate HR to a position of power and primacy in the organization, and make sure HR people have the special qualities to help managers build leaders and careers."

We recognize the importance of assigning the status required and developing the knowledge and skills of those in these positions.

Training Needs—First Line Supervisors and Group Leaders

These people feel as though they operate in a vice. There is constant pressure from management for increased productivity, high product quality, cost reduction, on-time shipments, and employee safety. The supervisor is expected to be positive, persuasive and personable. The supervisor also applies contract provisions, personnel and employee compliance with policies, procedures and safety legislation. Just one more thing—the paperwork—the endless paperwork—they live under the mantra of "Get it done now!"

It should be no surprise that these participants in training courses are impatient and intolerant of trainers who have had no personal or practical leadership experience. Lecturing and Power-Point presentations are considered boring and at times remind them of unpleasant school days. A trainer who relies on the presentation of concepts and theories loses the attention and interest of the group rapidly. What gets them excited and embroiled is discussion of practical issues and experiences and how to deal with common problems such as absenteeism, overtime scheduling, drug abuse, corrective discipline and dealing with unruly and challenging employees.

But we expect the first line supervisor to deal with these issues and meet the deadlines and production needs on time. Many of these same difficulties are now being experienced in office situations.

Determining Training Needs

The best method to determine training needs is to have the trainer/facilitator do a pre-course interview with each person and their manager. This generates useful information that these people may hesitate to share in any other way.

In many situations, using more than one method greatly adds to the value of the information and therefore the resulting decisions. The following practices are all useful. (The choice depends on the size of the group to be trained, whether centralized or dispersed, accessibility, time availability and budget.)

- Select from a variety of questionnaires, checklists, or surveys. Online surveys can make the process of administering, collecting and analyzing results quick and easy.

- Use senior management and LDT member interviews to provide input as to the importance of certain needs to the organization. With this, you are also considering their opinions and intuition about needs.

- Consider the opinions and intuition of the outside facilitator or consultant.

- Include operating reports where relevant as they provide measurable data that indicates the size and extent of a problem/opportunity. (This indicates the value of correcting the problem.)

Operating Indicators Point to Potential Goldmines

There are other clear sources of information on training needs that are often not tapped. As a result, this valuable information is lost when determining needs and developing a training response. Here are a few examples:

Example #1: Most have heard of Sam Walton the founder of Wal-Mart, and his dedication to personally visiting as many stores as possible each week. This practice has been labeled MBWA—Management by Walking Around. We have commented on the practice earlier. It is not the walking around that is significant—it's what is learned.

In the division of a diversified automotive parts producer, the general manager toured the complete facilities each morning. Then he returned to his office and called his superintendents asking why there was so much scrap in this department, employee absenteeism in another and idle equipment in another. He knew that when there is scrap, there is lost production which usually has to be made up with overtime—an additional cost. Similarly, absenteeism restricts productivity, as does equipment which is not operating. He knew the daily performance issues without hard copy reports or his computer screen.

Example #2:

In some organizations, the indicators are in the customer service department. This is the repository of customer complaints, product returns, refunds, replacements and warranty claims. All are costs that are unnecessary and all affect profitability. All are indicators of errors made somewhere in the production or delivery process and not rectified before shipment.

Also, companies that have quality departments usually accumulate and report what is termed the "Cost of Quality." Every element of cost incurred because a product was not produced, shipped or billed correctly the first time is calculated. Philip Crosby estimated that in many companies this figure may be as much as 15% of revenues or more; an excellent opportunity for profit improvement. Our experience is that in some organizations this number reaches 25% and in some, the numbers are deliberately understated to avoid management action. This type of cover-up eliminates action to seize these opportunities for improvement and cost reduction. A terrible situation!

Training people who leave the comfort of their offices to tour such areas and speak to the leaders will soon discover potential goldmines. The HR person and the trainer can assist in solving problems that are felt needs, relevant and significant. In this way they gain credibility and support.

Toronto to Tampa: Cranberry Martinis and a Trainee Talks

Opportunities for research are everywhere! In the process of writing this book, a trip to Toronto, Canada became necessary. It was on the return trip to Tampa, Florida that such an opportunity presented itself.

A group of four people boarded the plane just ahead of me. Their seats, all aisle seats, were obviously chosen so they could chat easily with each other during the flight. Mine was a window seat with an unoccupied middle seat beside me, and one of the four people, a young woman was in the aisle seat. She settled in, stowed her purse and when the flight attendant circulated she ordered a cranberry martini. After a few words with her cohorts and several sips of the cocktail, she expelled a deep sigh and obviously relaxed.

Being naturally curious, searching for content for the book and to break the boredom of the trip, I leaned over and asked, "Is your group off to a conference or training event in Tampa?"

She replied, "There are four of us from a major leasing corporation and we'll be in Tampa for a three-day sales conference." Offering her hand to shake she said, "My name is Monique." In turn, I introduced myself and mentioned that I was working on a second book.

Naturally she asked, "What's the topic?"

I replied, "It's about using training as a catalyst for developing individuals and at the same time achieving organizational goals. It's something like learning to golf. You take basic group golf lessons, then play a few times and then take a few lessons from the pro to improve your game and over time you become better and better at it. Then, you invite clients or potential associates to play and the golf outings becomes a channel for developing friendships and sometimes long term relationships." I asked, "Does that make sense to you?"

"I'm in sales," she said, "and it makes perfect sense."

Sensing openness, I asked "Would you help me by answering a few questions about your training experiences?" She agreed immediately while ordering a second cranberry martini.

Cocktail in hand, she said, "Fire away with your questions."

Since you are in sales, let me ask, "What sales training have you received with the company?" Just before she could answer, I said, "Hold it, before you answer, let me be more specific. I don't mean product/ service knowledge training, I mean selling skills."

"Well," she responded, "we did participate is a training course that taught us a five step sales process to guide us in our face-to-face contacts with clients."

Of course I asked, "Did you feel it was useful? Was it something you could apply?"

She replied, "Yes, it helped me follow a track so I didn't wander off course or forget an important step."

"How long ago was that?" I pursued.

She responded saying, "It was three years ago and we have not had any additional skills training since." When asked what she liked about the training, she replied, "What I thought was great was the fact that they invited our customer service reps to participate with us and they mixed us together during small group discussions. This gave us each a better understanding of how important it is to support each other. My suggestion would be that companies do something like this at least once a year, it would pay off not only in better co-operation but also in happier customers and more sales closed. Even more important was learning that selling is a process of inter-acting with the client and there are effective methods of doing that. Learn-ing that, made me feel more focused, confident and more professional."

Spontaneously, I decided on an informal test. After two martinis Monique would likely answer a tougher question, so I asked, "Monique can you remember the five steps in the process?"

She squirmed a bit, and frowned a little but finally admitted, "No I can't remember the exact words but I sense what I should do and say."

Not wanting to embarrass her, I let this go, but continued by asking, "Monique, you've shared what you liked most about the training and I appreciate that. Your answers make sense and are helpful. Please tell me a couple of things the company could do to improve their training efforts?"

"Because you asked about the five steps, what comes to mind first is that no one ever held us accountable for learning or using the five steps. I wish they would have." She continued, "It makes it seem that my boss doesn't care; that it's not important. The training itself and going through it with others was such a great and motivational experience. Then with no further follow-up it becomes de-motivational. It makes me think a little less of those in charge and respect their ability and commitment less."

"As I think about it," Monique continued, "why did they wait for three years before providing this training? It was so good and so useful I should have had it much sooner and would have been successful sooner."

She now lapsed into a thoughtful pause, then continued with, "There is one other suggestion. Several of my friends are in sales with other companies and they have had courses that are more advanced, that go beyond the basic sales process. Courses in how to interpret body language, using certain words and phrases which influence the buyer positively and how to negotiate effectively and other techniques," she explained. "Ours is a sales driven organization. The success of the company and its profitability is determined by our sales volume and our ability to hold our margins, so why don't they do more to develop our abilities?"

Had we asked her what percentage of the market her company had, she likely would have answered somewhere less than half. Therefore, the unachieved potential business was in the millions of dollars. With this amount available would there have been any doubt about whether or not to invest additional funds in sales training? We think not. Increases in sales volume usually generate incredible profit increases.

Thanking Monique again for her input I promised to use what I could in the book. After a few minutes, Monique slipped into a blissful martini-induced nap.

Determining the Value of Potential Bounty

Could Monique have increased her sales volume? She believed she could. She wanted to and would have participated. The barrier to achieving this gain resides in the mind of the sales manager, her Unit Leader. This manager (or the president) was focused on training cost rather than on maximizing market share, sales per person, and the resulting profit gains. This is an example of accepting "good enough" rather than pursuing "great."

If management had analyzed current market share and sales per person, then calculated the financial gains which could accrue from a modest 5% or 10% increase, they would have realized there was virtually no downside risk and significant upside profit potential. This analogy highlights the payback available from advanced training and the need for reminders and refreshers to ensure retention and continued application of the knowledge.

Observations: Developing a dynamic and effective organization requires a thoughtful, planned series of purposefully chosen training and developmental activities:

- Including all members of a natural work team in the training sessions builds the effectiveness and cohesiveness of the teams.

- There are certain skills that every person requires and which should be scheduled soon after or just before they are assigned to new duties.

- Follow-up training that builds on what has been done before reinforces the previous training and builds to a higher level of competency and achievement.

- Dynamic companies often choose training as one of their most important catalysts for coping with change, solving problems and preparing for opportunities.

    There are impressive gains available in organizations, untapped because of a negative focus on costs rather than on the pursuit of potential gains. Some leaders, inadvertently and unintentionally limit the success of the organization and the people in it by this mindset.

Ovation Automotive: the Story Continues... the Team Identifies the Training Needs

In the previous chapter, we learned that the president responsible for five manufacturing plants had formed his Leadership Development Team. As stated in Best Practice Two they began identifying needs. They decided that surveys, personal interviews or focus groups were unnecessary. Rather they used their own abbreviated process: the opinions and intuition of senior management including input from the president, manager of continuous improvement, training manager, and the most progressive of their five plant managers.

The team completed a brief situation analysis and five primary factors determined their need for training:

1. Rapid growth had required the appointment of many new supervisors.

2. There had been no previous training. Supervisors had been expected to learn by trial and error. That was proving too costly and unacceptable.

3. Employee grievances were increasing because of the supervisors' lack of knowledge and skill in supervisory techniques.

4. Scrap and the replacement costs were escalating due to the inability of supervisors and managers to stem the problems and solve the root causes.

5. There was no doubt on the part of this team that there was an urgent need for improvement.

The Plan: In developing a training program, they made key decisions and identified their criteria:

- They wanted practical, real-life training for their first line supervisors. They did not want an off-the-shelf generic program or one that was developed for white-collar supervisors—definitely not something academic and conceptual.

- The terminology, topics and methods had to be particularly geared to manufacturing and as much as possible to the automotive industry specifically.

- This course would be the foundation on which future training would be built. Newly appointed supervisors in future would participate in the same training to develop a common base of knowledge, skill and terminology.

- Finally, the trainer/facilitators had to have, as a minimum, a working knowledge of automotive manufacturing and preferably actual experience.

Ovation's Progress Report

(Progress is rated in terms of Grim, Good, Great or To Be Determined)

Great: They were clear and concise in describing their needs.

- It was obvious that they knew the situation and what needed to be done.

- Setting the criteria for the training at this stage was a useful guide as they pursued their goal.

Grim: No effort was made or considered to identify their expectations in terms of behavioral change, application, or measurable results.

To Be Determined: Additional analysis may have been helpful in identifying specific areas and specific improvements. More would have been gained had they clearly spelled out the responsibility of the superintendent in ensuring application and results.

Finally: They recognized the needs, took prompt action and did it as a team. Certainly an abbreviated but appropriate application of Best Practice Two.

You'll learn more about this company's
progress in the following chapters.

Application of These Ideas

The most significant ideas in this chapter for me were:

_____

As a result, I intend to:

_____

A Question for You:

Shouldn't every supervisor, manager and executive know why employees don't do what is expected? If the answer is "yes," order the book *Employees Not Doing What You Expect* at EmployeesNotDoingWhatYouExpect.com.

Action Prompt:

- Start a file labeled "Training Needs and Potential Gains." Once you open this folder, selective perception will take effect and more ideas and information will automatically attract your attention.

- Which training needs identification methods are used in your organization now?

  _____

- Which should be added or deleted in future?

  _____

- Test the value of walking around intentionally to identify problem/opportunities. Then note below what you experienced.

  _____

In the next section, we'll focus on how-to chose the optimal trainer/facilitator fully in line with training needs and goals.

Chapter 5

Best Practice Three

Select a Trainer/Facilitator Best Able to Achieve the Predetermined Outcomes

Reason: The facilitator is a vital link, generating the knowledge, skills and understanding for participants and providing feedback and suggestions to the Leadership Development Team.

INSPIRE

The growth and development of people is the highest calling of leadership.

–Harvey S. Firestone

Best Practice Three

Select a trainer/facilitator with skills and methods
best able to achieve the predetermined
goals and outcomes.

The Details: The LDT's function at this juncture is to establish selection criteria, and evaluate potential candidates on the basis of proven capability and credibility both at senior levels and with the intended participants. This person must also have the ability and confidence to deal with potential challenges.

Participants quickly realize whether a facilitator is genuine and knowledgeable in both theory and practice and whether is relates to their work environment. The question is whether the potential trainer/facilitator has *walked the talk,* or simply presents generic theories developed by others. They become frustrated and impatient with facilitators who lecture participants on *what to do* in general terms and *why* conceptually, but are unable to demonstrate *how to do it* in regards to the practical application of the concepts.

The Benefits: Having the LDT determine training goals and evaluate potential candidates ensures impact and fit. It also ensures future support. The following are three credibility and career damaging experiences that companies have had that you and your team need to avoid.

The Situation at Titan Transportation Equipment: Having determined a training need for their first line plant supervisors, the HR specialist contacted the local community college and asked them to provide both a course and the facilitator. They left the relevant decisions up to those at the college.

After the second session, participants complained to HR saying, "This person does nothing but read to us from a book; we could do that ourselves." Asking a few questions, the HR manager learned that the college had chosen a person who instructed their evening extension course in supervision and there had been no complaints. More surprising was that the instructor was a labor relations manager for a mid-sized manufacturing company and therefore, had relevant experience he could have shared.

The Results: The program was canceled, the credibility of the HR department was eroded, supervisors were not trained, money was wasted and the problems continued.

Observations: This trainer had valuable labor relations experience but lacked the training, facilitation skills and the personality to relate to these people.

- Some facilitators are acceptable to participants attending a course to earn a certificate or diploma because they are not concerned about *can do* abilities.

- Colleges and universities are fine educational institutions. However, their instructors and methods may not be relevant to participants and their employers who expect application and results.

The Situation at Diesel Division: A group of 15 managers were selected to attend a motivational management course, which was being conducted by corporate trainers at an off-site location. During the two-hour drive to the hotel, Lloyd, the plant superintendent, and I (a participant rather than a facilitator) discussed our expectations.

It was agreed that if the course became boring, we would provoke discussion by arguing opposing viewpoints. Further, we would take turns either agreeing or disagreeing with the facilitators. One day, Lloyd would take the positive position, and the next day I would. This worked well and seemed to have gone undetected. However, at the conclusion of the course the facilitators shook hands and knowingly thanked us for our actions.

The Results: The program was completed, and participants learned interesting concepts and principles. However, many felt it was a waste because there was no effort to develop skills or discuss application. There was a substantial training investment but little change took place. Opportunity was lost and funds wasted. They wanted answers and received only concepts.

Observations: Both facilitators were capable and likeable people. However, they had been trained as teachers and therefore used presentations rather than interactive methods. Finally, while they led participants through the Hawthorne Experiments, Maslow's Hierarchy of Needs, and McGregor's Theory X and Y Management beliefs, they were unable to translate these concepts into practical on-the-job suggestions because they lacked actual leadership experience. Therefore, they failed in creating useful new behaviors and skills.

The Situation at Brentwood Power: At Brentwood Power, John Stewart had made a risky and difficult decision. He informed his manager that the corporate trainer they had assigned to deliver workshops at his location was not effective.

When John first called his manager with the complaint he received a skeptical response. "No one else has complained," his manager insisted, thinking that possibly it was John and his staff who were lacking, not the trainer.

John asked, "Have you or any of the other executives personally seen this trainer in action?" John's boss hemmed and hawed, then reluctantly admitted that they had not. John suggested that they attend a session nearby to check for themselves.

A few days later, the verdict was in and the trainer was out. "We had no idea he was so ineffective," John's boss admitted. When the executive had called John's counterparts at other locations he discovered that there was wide agreement that the training was disappointing and unacceptable.

Evidently the trainer was recruited two years before. In the interim, he had delivered courses to more than one hundred shift leaders, supervisors and managers at eighteen sites. When asked why they didn't report their concerns, they said that since it was a corporate initiative they felt that they had a duty to accept it. Also, they could show it as a goal completed.

The Results: Subsequently the trainer's contract was terminated. Now a new program was underway with a new facilitator and John was hearing positive comments from the participants and seeing results. He knew he had made the right decision.

What John and the other Brentwood site managers had experienced was a trainer who was egocentric, telling outlandish stories of personal accomplishments and attempting to impress his audience with his vast knowledge. He listened little. The training methods were too long and boring to hold the group's attention. Some trainees had accepted the trainer's delivery as it was, because they had little with which to compare. Others simply endured it because it was a corporate initiative. The content of the modules addressed the needed topics. It was just that the delivery was so dry, boring and dragged out that the trainees felt little interest or motivation to use what was presented.

Observations: Trainers are not all created equal—be careful about who you entrust to deliver such services to your organization. It could impact your personal credibility and the viability of future initiatives.

Trainer/Facilitator Selection—Avoid the Traps

When interviewing and choosing a trainer/facilitator, these are some of the common traps and mistakes made by those in the position of hiring that can have costly results and lead to disappointment:

a. **The Credentials Trap:** The candidate has impressive credentials from one or more respected institutions, which creates a great impression—but lack essential elements listed earlier. For example, one organization desperately needed a knowledgeable person to prepare materials for an upcoming management course. They located a person pursuing his PhD in Instructional Design who was available and wanted the assignment. The flawed results were due to the person using academic terminology, as though preparing a paper for a professor, rather than commonly used language that participants could relate to.

b. **The Experience Trap:** A candidate may have experience in compensation and benefits, salaried administration, HR planning or health and safety and be adept in these areas. However, none of these abilities necessarily demonstrates an ability to facilitate leadership training. It may qualify them to do presentations to certain employee groups in their area of expertise. Unfortunately, these individuals tend to lecture or use presentation methods which may impart information, but do not develop understanding or skills.

c. **The Halo Effect**: The candidate has one or more traits or elements, which impress the assessor to the exclusion of other aspects and deficiencies. For example, an attractive appearance and likeable personality are certainly desirable factors but not as important as facilitation skills.

d. **A Friend/HR Association Acquaintance**: As in those above, this person may have a wonderful personality and certain experience and capabilities, but can they facilitate leadership training that produces measurable results?

e. **The Egotist**: This candidate likely has many of the credentials listed in the first item, is a member of several associations and may sit on community committees. Their resumes tend to be detailed. In the interview, they do most of the talking and ask few questions. Beware, the egotist has little regard for others' needs and emphasizes resume content to mask personality quirks and lack of relating ability.

f. **The Want-To-Be**: There are those who aspire to be motivational speakers, or trainers/facilitators—yet haven't proven themselves in the field. In some cases, they are teachers and want to make a career change. Some have joined Toastmasters, taken a Dale Carnegie course and now feel ready to become facilitator/trainers. Unfortunately they may lack the business knowledge and leadership experience to be effective with supervisory/management participants.

Trainer/Facilitator Selection Criteria and Evaluation

(Use this form for both internal & external candidates)

Out of 100 points, assign a portion of the points to each element in the column. First, in terms of importance to achieving the required outcomes. Second, score the candidate on how well their factors seem to meet the requirements. If uncertain, use a question mark and note the uncertainty in the comments section below.

Candidate Name_____ Date_____

Element	Importance	Candidate Score
1. Relevant Experience:		
a. Training/facilitation/coaching		
b. Supervisory/management/leadership		
c. Business/industry/other	_____	_____
2. Personality:		
Friendly, positive, energetic, expressive	_____	_____
3. Credentials:		
Business, education, training	_____	_____
4. Appearance:		
Neat, businesslike, and appropriate	_____	_____
5. Special and Significant:		
a. Ability to relate to the Unit leader, HR, LMs and participants		
b. Coaching skills & experience		
c. Process & results focus		
d. Ability to confront and resolve potential issues with tact	_____	_____
Total (/100):		

Will this person relate to our people at all levels on the basis of credibility, competence and personality? Will he/she be able to achieve the required outcomes?

*Comments:*_____

_____

Additional Facilitator Assessment Methods

In addition to the assessment scale, here are some additional key elements we've discovered and used to choose the optimal person:

- Schedule a personal interview with members of the LDT— remembering that the successful candidate will become a temporary member of the LDT.

- Do background, reference and credential checks.

- View the final candidates in an actual training/facilitation situation.

- Arrange to have this person conduct a training/facilitation demonstration for the LDT. (Don't be miserly, be fair and compensate the candidate for time and transportation.)

Consider Methods and Materials

There is no doubt that choosing the best facilitator is of primary importance in ensuring course success.

An integral part of the facilitator's effectiveness is based on their techniques and materials. Therefore, it is important to determine their planned methods and preview their intended materials. Research confirms that the following are the **most effective** with adult participants:

- Learning is most effective when it is linked with the participants' existing knowledge and experiences.

- Methods that allow and encourage participant discussion, practice and other interactive methods increase both motivation, and their ability to apply what they have learned. Plus they learn from the most capable others in the group— an important and credible source of expertise.

- Therefore, small group discussion about typical problems, needed improvements or upcoming changes and related projects and exercises are the very best. Having participants document specific examples of where and when they applied course content and the end results, encourages application.

- Participants pay particular attention when a senior manager attends and points out how this content and learning are linked to current and future initiatives.

- Lectures/presentations delivered to "passive" participants are boring and **least effective** unless followed by discussion, practice and reminders.

In addition, to assess the fit and effectiveness of a trainer/facilitator's instruction style, consider the following research findings on how adults actually learn:

10% of what we read: The fact is that fewer people are reading books and newspapers. Therefore, materials used should be minimal, relevant and geared to the trainees' reading level. A great tool is providing "reminder cards" or a similar condensed summary that are pocket-sized for ready reference.

20% of what we hear: When we are listening, our minds often tune-in and out. A boring speaker is quickly tuned out. Effective facilitators find interesting ways to repeat key ideas several times often referred to as "spaced repetition."

30% of what we see: Our attention is stimulated by movement and images. Facial expressions, and hand gestures (think "body language") when used appropriately will increase impact. The use of models, videos, reenactments and other visual methods can support the learning.

50% of what we see and hear: Two senses are engaged and result in increased retention.

70% of what we say as we talk: This not only engages our senses but our mind. Small group discussion can assist greatly here.

90% of what we say as we do something: Our mind is involved in thinking and we are using our motor skills as well.

Retention is further increased by repetition. Advertisers have learned that frequent reminders even when annoying, build product awareness, name retention and they influence future purchase decisions.

Caution: When reviewing training proposals from potential providers, look beyond the bullet points that describe the modules. Creating fancy titles and good brochure copy is relatively simple. Delivering training in a way that impacts behavior and corresponding results is much more challenging. It depends to a high degree on the trainer's approach, personality and skills.

> **Keep in Mind: The most expensive isn't always the best.**
>
> **The cheapest isn't always the worst.**
>
> **Focus on who can achieve the best results.**
>
> **Provide that person with the time and support required to maximize impact.**

The following are some in-the-field examples that illustrate this third Best Practice point of selecting a trainer/facilitator and methods that are best able to achieve the predetermined goals and desired outcomes.

The Situation at National Petrol Products—A Key Question: It has been said that there are two words, when spoken, even in a crowded room are likely to be heard above the din of conversation. Those words are *our own name* and the other is the word *sex*. Our hearing is finely tuned towards certain words and phrases.

> **Tip: *Profitability* is such a word for CEO's, presidents, and in fact for most executives. When you want their attention and interest, use the word *profitability* in your presentation. Also powerful are the words—faster, cheaper, better.**

With the next client, this wasn't necessary. The HR manager called and asked, "Do you people do sales training that is directed towards improved profitability?" That key question lead to one of the most intensive and productive training events we have ever facilitated. The Unit Leader's challenges were spelled out at the first meeting as he articulated what he wanted to accomplish.

The general manager came right to the point saying, "In this lubricants and greases division for which I'm responsible, we have been selling our products as commodities and have used price as the primary reason to buy. Initially this was helpful because we needed to increase volume to achieve critical mass. But now we have to change focus. We have to sell value and higher margin solutions for customer problems." He continued, "Our sales people must become more involved in recommending the best product to meet the customer's performance requirements. Many do this now, but after all of this effort and expertise, they still feel they have to quote the lowest price to win the business. That's the crux of our challenge," he said emphatically jabbing his finger in the air. Now that he had started he was energized and began pacing as he spoke. "I'll be brutally frank. This division is threatened with being sold if profit margins are not brought up to acceptable levels soon."

He continued, "I was promoted to head this division a year ago and I know these people well. They are tops in product knowledge, application engineering and customer relationships. But they find it impossible to believe that we can charge more than our competitors and justify it. I've struggled with the problem, trying to determine a solution. Finally I've decided that we are going to provide them with sales training, but it needs to be focused on value-based selling. Once this is completed, we will evaluate the degree of change and decide what to do next. But we aren't going to give up until we get this done."

Turning on his heel, he pointed his finger and challengingly asked, "Can you do this for us?"

Pausing for a moment, the reply was, "If you are asking can we do the sales training, the answer is yes and we can customize the content to reflect what your sales people actually have to do to be successful. But if you are asking, can we change their behaviors so that they quote higher prices and close sales at these higher levels, my answer is we can't do that alone. But we can help you and your managers and sales people so that together the result is achieved."

The Solution: "Good," he said, "let's get the show on the road. Our training manager and one of our sales managers will be your contact points. They will check your credentials, discuss specific customized content and review your proposal. Then they will work with you in determining how the content will be applied and any other actions we need to take to ensure our goals are achieved. By the way, build into your proposal a meeting with the four of us once a month to monitor progress and ensure results."

Within two months the basic training was completed. At the monthly meeting it was determined that both the participants and the manager wanted another session. This additional session was to be an intensive simulation exercise. They wanted to 1) role-play typical customer contacts, complete with presentations, and 2) watch our facilitator role-playing what they were expected to say and do.

We had to quickly learn the basics of their products and methods. Further because the team wanted to elevate their abilities they developed even tougher requirements. This included having both new and seasoned sales people from different regions and various markets make a variety of sales presentations. To increase the realism, each team would be evaluated on the basis of their presentation to a purchasing group. These buyers were trained to act out their roles according to the case studies. Each team had access to the marketing materials and literature that would normally be used. In addition, it was necessary to update the company Customer Relationship Management system. CRM as it is referred to, is used by sales personnel to input customer information that assists in tracking sales results and new opportunities.

During these simulations, once the teams had made their presentation to the buying group, they had to successfully negotiate a final business relationship. As you can imagine, the participants were extremely nervous but at the same time they wanted to know how to sell value, how to do what their GM and sales managers required and how to prove themselves as value-sellers.

It was an intensive white-knuckle three days but hour-by-hour their confidence increased through watching the facilitator demonstrate, observing each other perform and through the experience gained in doing their own presentations.

The Profitable Results: Their excitement and enthusiasm grew and by the end of the final session it could no longer be contained. The group spontaneously stood and gave themselves a standing ovation!

**When you have well-planned focused training
with simulations, plus participation and
coaching by managers it creates a synergism
that achieves and exceeds desired results.**

For this group, it was the participation of the product sales mangers and coaching by other managers that produced both tangible profit margin improvement and intangible self-confidence and camaraderie that flows through their entire sphere of influence. A reminder, the key word again is *profitability*. With increased skill and by surviving a tough challenge, success is the result that continues to grow. In addition, there was a final benefit. Subsequently, the fuels division also applied these methods with rapid and lasting results.

Return to Ovation Automotive—The Story Continues

As we continue with our ongoing real life examples from Ovation Automotive, we find that having determined their needs, the LDT now had to decide who would do the training. To his credit, the newly recruited training manager, Tony shared his feelings that he was not ready to do this training and that he needed further experience. However, he had made some contacts and felt that a company in the region was of a size, and had the appropriate experience and background to be considered. Further, he learned that our company was facilitating a one-day conference in the area, where they could attend to evaluate our effectiveness and meet us personally.

Three Mysterious Men on a Mission: *Seven Proven Methods for Improving Performance and Productivity* was the title of the seminar we were conducting. Three of the Ovation team enrolled and attended. They were Bill the vice president of manufacturing, Tony the training manager and George the manager of continuous improvement.

They participated little but conferred amongst themselves. At lunch they sat separately and at the afternoon coffee break, approached, shook hands and said they were leaving. The only departing words were, "We've learned what we needed, give us a call next week." They left without further explanation. Who were these people we wondered?

When we called Bill, the V.P. of manufacturing, he simply said, "We've been looking for a firm to train 50 first-line supervisors. After seeing you folks in action, we think you can do the job. Give Tony, our training manager, a call and he will give you the details."

In contacting Tony, we found he was very direct and quickly outlined their situation. He advised us that so far the only training they've done was safety training, a short session on handling grievances, and another on quality methods. What they needed was a leadership course that would provide the foundation for all future training. It should include an overview of supervisory responsibilities and some basic skill building to develop the capability and confidence of these supervisors. In addition he outlined major challenges, and said he'd get back to us soon after he received our proposal.

Ovation's Progress Report

(Progress is rated in terms of Grim, Good, Great or To Be Determined)

Great: Having the LDT members evaluate the potential trainer/facilitator(s), the company and their other related capabilities proved effective, established consensus and ensured subsequent approval.

The critical decision regarding use of their internal trainer or external resources was made with the concurrence of the training manager. In some cases this might have become a challenge to the internal person's ego, but not at Ovation.

Attending the seminar as a group also provided the training manager with an opportunity to observe, learn and compare his own capability.

Grim: At this point the team still had not established outcome expectations. This was done almost as an afterthought, as we will see in the next chapter.

Finally: The team has made an important decision and one that is significant to the eventual success to the efforts. They have been effective even though they were unaware of Best Practice Three.

The Ovation story continues in the following chapters.

Application of Best Practice Three

In this chapter on selecting a facilitator/trainer and their methods, the key ideas for me were:

_____

As a result I intend to:

_____

Action Prompt:

- Keep this book on your desk, it will remind you of your intentions and stimulate your selective-perception.

- In your opinion, how could your organization improve its trainer/facilitator selection process?

_____

Remember the 'Facilitator Selection Checklist' found in this chapter.
For your own free copy, please visit our website FusionorFizzle.com

Chapter 6

Best Practice Four

Crystallize and Communicate the Expectations

Reason: When you consider and clearly communicate all expectations—especially in regards to results, intangibles, indicators of success and consequences–it provides essential information to all participants and those who support them regarding the purpose and outcomes. It instills reality and provides both challenge and accountability, which are highly motivational factors.

If your actions inspire others to dream more, learn more, do more and become more, you are a leader.

–John Quincy Adams

INSPIRE

Best Practice Four

Crystallize, focus and communicate the expectations.

The word "crystallize" is a powerful one that not only sums up the intention of Best Practice Four, but the energy of the action needed as well.

The Details: The Leadership Development Team (LDT) with other significant decision makers defines the expectations in terms of changes in knowledge, skills, participation, application, behavior changes and results. By doing this, those involved are able to focus on the solutions rather than the roadblocks to their training success. Here are some aspects to consider while in this process:

- Explain why these outcomes are important to the organization, to the individual participants and to their managers.

- Identify the indicators that will be used to determine progress and success. Consider using regular operating reports and observable behaviors for these indicators.

- Determine and apply appropriate consequences for those who contribute and for those who could do so but choose not to make the effort required.

- Promote deep communication of the expectations throughout the organization to ensure that everyone gets the message.

Certain employees test the resolve and seriousness of management. Some see it as a test of wills. It is the, "You can't make me," behavior we at times see in children and teens. Some act automatically while others consider it the reality check of management's resolve.

> **Expectations may be tested. To circumvent and prevent going off course, plan appropriate and positive responses and consequences— and communicate them early.**

While many participants conscientiously complete all assignments, endeavor to build their skills and apply them effectively, a few others do little to learn or develop their skills. In fact, a few consciously and deliberately flaunt the fact that they are doing nothing. They wait to see if anyone cares or takes any action whatsoever. In some companies nothing is done and management loses respect and credibility. Eventually, more employees follow the same pattern until it becomes the norm and part of the organizational culture.

In others, the employee needs to be cautioned and if there is no improvement in their behavior with further corrective action taking place that may finally lead to their replacement. When doing this, everyone must clearly understand the expectations and the consequences. Fortunately, there is a wide range of consequences that are less drastic and usually effective in achieving compliance.

At Electronic Security Systems Inc.

At this international branch plant with almost 200 employees, the general manager launched a leadership course by explaining his beliefs about how it would benefit those attending and contribute to the future growth of the company. He asked for their commitment and best efforts and wished them well.

The Situation at Electronic Security Systems Inc.: At the first session, of the 22 scheduled participants (all engineers and technicians), only three were on time for the start. The balance straggled in over the next twenty minutes and the last participant arrived 90 minutes late. With judicious questioning after the session, we learned that this behavior was normal for the group. Rarely was anyone on time for any meeting in this organization.

The Solution: Faced with this problem, the Unit Leader was asked and did advise everyone again that being on time was important and expected. At the same time, we prepared a chart titled *On Time Performance*. Participant names were listed on the left and the session numbers across the top and it was posted prominently at the front of the conference room. As people arrived on time, a check was marked beside their name. For those arriving late, a number indicating the number of minutes late was shown.

The Results: At the next session, all but three were on time. At future sessions all but one, were there. It was her habit to always be late. Some thought that it was because of her high self-opinion. But that is only a supposition.

Observations: When a person fails to attend or complete assignments or to apply and report, it is important to not ignore the lapse. The first step is simply to say, "We missed you or we noticed that your assignment wasn't completed, is there a problem I can help you with?" Give them time to answer. Then ask, "Do you need some one-on-one coaching?" If the answer is no, proceed by asking, "Can I count on you to participate fully in the remaining sessions, as it's important."

- Usually, this action will end the unacceptable behavior promptly. However, if there is no intervention or consequences, the behavior is seen as acceptable and tends to spread to other people and other activities.

Why Don't Employees Do what is Expected?

In our book titled, *Employees Not Doing What You Expect,* the twelve most frequent reasons for non-compliance were listed. The first reason cited was that employees don't know *what is expected*, and the third reason is they don't know *how to do it*. We found that when asked *why* and the answer often is, "No one told me or showed me what to do, or how to do it."

And then the question, "Why weren't they told and shown?" was asked, without a clear response. The answer indicates supervisors, managers and other leaders who are not fulfilling their basic duty, to ensure employee performance. The next question again obviously is, "Why, aren't those in leadership/management positions doing what they need to do to create a capable, dynamic and motivated workforce?" The answer is one of two reasons, either they *don't know how*—indicating a training need OR they *do know how* but are neglecting their responsibilities, a dereliction of duty. Are they MIA—Missing in Action—or prone to LOA—a Lack of Action?

Regardless of which is correct, the next *why* question is, "Why is this allowed to continue?"

Often the bluntest answer is, "Because the Unit Leader in charge is allowing it to continue." Remember: what we tolerate, we propagate. The leader in charge by his or her lack of action is permitting the situation to continue. Inevitably this lack of action creates a downward spiral affecting not only the performance of individuals, but eventually the bottom line performance of the organization, its customers and shareholders.

Decades of experience indicate that the greatest training need in most organizations is leadership/management training and development. This effort needs to begin with the Unit Leader and his or her direct reports. Some executives and their managers have impressive credentials from respected universities and colleges—but the fact is they either lack the capability—the know-how—to lead or the will to ensure performance. In fact, many professional schools that confer MBAs do not develop the *people skills* needed by most managers and supervisors.

Tip: Credentials do not guarantee capability, commitment or character. In fact, their years spent in pursuing their education has left little time for gaining actual on-the-job experience, and particularly people skills.

Observations: It is a significant key responsibility of every leader to personally ensure that employees and supervisors understand their responsibilities, are properly trained and can perform effectively. If able and available, the leader should do this personally. If not, use the HR/training personnel. If they in turn are not able or available, reach outside the company and utilize qualified external trainer/facilitators.

- To do nothing, is costly in financial terms, morale, and customer satisfaction.

  It should not be an option. It also erodes trust and respect for the leader.

- Too often training is done too little and too late, undermined by negative leadership beliefs, unfortunate past practices or self-limiting expectations.

- Employees cope by developing their own methods, which may be effective or detrimental. Regardless, these habits once established are difficult to alter.

- Some leaders expect too little, concerned that high expectations either cannot or will not be met, or that their participants will be resistant or de-motivated. These are negative beliefs. Just the opposite is true. Typically participants discuss with pride having successfully completed a tough course.

**Leaders tend to get what they
expect, express and exhibit.**

Situation at Polaris Logistics: Evan, the CEO chose to wait until the room was nearly empty to get our ear. First he wanted to shift our location and give us some background. He said, "Let's go to my office get the paperwork signed and get this training on the tracks." His words and body language signaled that something more significant was to be discussed.

"There is an issue that I think is vitally important to the success of this venture." he began. "As you know, we have said the purpose of this training is to develop our middle and front-line managers. We want them to become leaders in fact, by behavior, rather than simply by title."

"More specifically, we want them to take more initiative in decision-making and leadership. Most have been promoted from within, and therefore know how this particular business operates. In addition, most understand our values, which we take seriously. However, in the past two years we have undergone major changes. This was a family owned business with paternalistic management. Now it operates under a corporate culture. During this period we have grown from a fleet size of 1,200 vehicles on lease to almost 4,000 and from two branches to six. While this has been quite an achievement, our next move will be even greater. Our vision is to become a national player. These people will have to take us from where we are now, to where we intend to go. They may not realize it yet, but we are going to help them become more professional and proactive."

He continued, "They need exposure to current leadership techniques. Hopefully your people as an external resource can help us do that. Before I sign the go-ahead however, I have a question that's been on my mind for the last few days. I think it's vital."

Then his query: "My question is, what should I personally do to make this training most effective and to ensure that we see changed behaviors?

Let me go even further; what behaviors of mine do I need to change and which do our senior management team members need to exhibit so that we all are leaders by example? I realize that we will accomplish little if you people teach them new methods while we keep doing things the way we have in the past. The participants will no doubt, revert back to their present ingrained habits."

We were impressed and said so. "Too often we hear management say, '*They* need to change, *they* need training.' Later as we work with the participants, they point their fingers upwards and say that management should have taken this training first."

Evan replied, "I understand that. I've been one of those participants, and have used the same words," he confessed. "So let's get to work and lay out a plan that makes this effort totally successful." Together, the following commitment statement was developed to crystallize the expectations for those involved:

We the Senior Leadership Team...

1. **Will communicate the purpose of the training** (in terms of participant capabilities and organizational goals) and establish clear expectations (participation, learning, application and behavior) and identify the indicators of progress towards meeting the expectations.

2. **Will participate in every session** and will personally use the same methods so that we experience the challenge of changing and act as leaders by example.

3. **Will coach our people** and help them identify and understand their personal leadership styles—both strengths and areas for improvement.

4. **Will be prepared** to resolve any difficulties and issues and do it in a positive, supportive, manner.

5. **Will arrange and encourage additional assistance** by the trainer/facilitator(s) for those who request it.

6. **Will meet with the trainer/facilitator regularly** to review progress, problem-solve, take corrective action and ensure final success.

The last point was suggested by Evan himself in order to demonstrate his personal commitment. As you can imagine, this left no doubt as to his commitment, or that of his senior team. Were there times when they were challenged and uncomfortable? Yes, of course! There is no growth without some discomfort.

This example at Polaris Logistics and the next where we revisit Ovation Automotive, demonstrates two different approaches to defining expectations. Both were effective. You, no doubt, will find other methods to achieve the same outcome.

The Ovation Story Continues: The Expectations are Established

In the previous chapter, under Best Practice Three (choosing a trainer/facilitator), we left Ovation Automotive needing to make some decisions and establishing their expected outcomes. The team was in place, most urgent needs identified, and potential facilitator/trainers evaluated and selected. The Ovation effort seemed ready for launch and implementation. Inexplicably progress came to a standstill.

Tony explaining the reasons saying, "When we took the proposal to the president, he approved it but said that he wanted two things, first to meet with you to discuss his expectations for this training. Second, he wanted these plans and arrangements presented to the five plant managers."

In addition—almost as an afterthought—Tony relayed the president's insistence, "Why don't you make this a special meeting and invite the labor relations manager, the V.P. of finance, and even the superintendents who report to the plant managers?"

"What a great opportunity to communicate what we are doing, how we are going to go about it and why it's important. It should also generate co-operation and support. I will be there as well," the president concluded. "Finally," he said, "it will also give us a chance to see these training people in action under some stress."

It was possibly the briefest meeting we ever attended. The president shook hands and congratulated us on our patience. Then he continued saying, "The last space shuttle launch in Florida reminded me that a launch is hailed as a great event and receives decent media coverage, but when the shuttle returns to earth successfully, it is accepted as routine. The reason I wanted to see you again along with Tony was to say that I want to launch this training initiative with fanfare. However, when we conclude this first effort, I want it to receive even greater attention. Be sure to provide an impressive course completion certificate for each person. Advise me of the date far enough ahead so I can attend. Allow time on the agenda so that I can shake each person's hand and present them with their certificate."

"Be sure to schedule about 15 minutes so that I can congratulate them and tell them about how this fits with our corporate competitive strategy and how it aligns with our vision and values. I want to end by telling them, how proud I am of their hard work and contribution to our success."

The requested management preview meeting was held a week later. It was a formidable group of 25 that assembled in the conference room. For most, this hadn't happened before. They were uncertain about what to expect and intrigued by the prospect.

Point-by-point, the president outlined the needs analysis and planning that had been done. He emphasized the reasons for training and that it was chosen because it was appropriate for their company and supervisors. To ensure this would be the case, he told them about the three managers who had attended the seminar to verify our capability and suitability. In conclusion he told them that there would be more training in the future and asked them to support these efforts and to co-operate in making their people available for the sessions.

Just before sitting down, he said, "By the way, please let me know when the training is completed, I want a meeting similar to this so we can discuss the results we achieved." This was his way of advising everyone that he personally would be involved and interested in the outcome.

At Ovation—The Bulldog Barks Again: We met him at our previous meetings at Ovation. The short, stocky plant manager, usually referred to as Bulldog. On this day he was at the presentation. It seemed to go well with the group being interested and positive. However, just as it was about to conclude, Bulldog asked questions that others should have been asking. They reflected his expectations and personality. He coughed and asked, "Just before we go, I have a question." He sounded innocent enough but it turned out to be a catalyst for change. "Actually, I have two questions," he continued. "Firstly, how will we know if our supervisors have learned anything? Second, how will we know if they can do what they've learned and that they will use it on the job?"

Later we learned that Bob had rightfully earned the nickname Bulldog. He was the most senior of the plant managers and built like the proverbial brick outhouse. The others were listening intently for the answers. He was right on the mark in asking these questions. They were relevant and deserved answers. In fact more organizations should ask them.

"You see," we responded, "in some organizations, tangible results or even behavior changes aren't a concern as long as participants enjoy the sessions. They think that just the fact that the participants attend the sessions will build co-operation, trust and teamwork."

"Well that's just not good enough for us." Bulldog said, emphasizing his words with a loud thump on the table.

"In that case, we could incorporate a written test as part of the course. However, to reinforce the elements you want them to learn and to avoid playing 'gotcha' we can have them write the test at the first session, and score it and then use the same test at the end of the course. That way they know what's expected and it should motivate them to learn. How do you feel about that?" we asked.

Bulldog answered with only one word, "Good," and another loud rap on the table.

We continued, "Now for your second question, which was, will they use and apply what they've learned. Without asking, we know this is important to you as well. This company is making a considerable investment not only financially, but also in the time participants will spend at the sessions and away from their departments. Since you want application and results, we have a solution that should appeal to you. A requirement can be included that each supervisor or participant tackles a specific pre-determined project as part of this course. Best of all, they will be directed to discuss their potential projects and final selection with their superintendent. Last, but not by any means least, they will be required to prepare a brief written report of their project results and present it verbally at the final session. To top it all off, all plant managers, superintendents and the president will be invited to attend that session."

Bulldog's head was nodding in agreement and this time he exploded with, "Fantastic, that's what I want to see happen." A third solid thump on the table shook the water glasses.

Now it was our turn to ask questions and the first was, "If this training is as important as you folks say, and I have no doubt that it is, why is it that only the production supervisors are scheduled to attend the course? To maximize the results, and co-operation shouldn't the supervisors from material control, quality and maintenance be involved as well?"

Bulldog hesitated only a second before saying, "Of course they should."

Continuing, we asked, "Since this is new to the company, with new methods and terminology, shouldn't the general supervisors be on board as well so they gain the same knowledge and are able to coach their supervisors in applying the methods?"

As the senior plant manager, and by his nature, it was obvious that Bulldog was taking the lead for the whole group and he again answered, "Yes, of course they should."

The momentum was seemingly unstoppable and the next question was, "What about the five superintendents?" In response to this and to orient and involve the superintendents, monthly content preview sessions were scheduled for all five of them.

With all of the key decision makers present, it seemed an opportune time to obtain one last decision and determine the extent of their resolve. It was reiterated that there was an agreement to pre- and post-tests of knowledge to determine what attendees have gained. The question was what did participants need to score to pass. The agreement was that their post-test score should be 90% as the participants would know the questions in advance. This number is indicative of the extent of the resolve and importance of the training.

Ovation's Progress Report

(Progress is rated in terms of Grim, Good, Great or To Be Determined)

Great: The idea of a presentation to the larger management group was an excellent method of sharing progress up to this point and the reasons for pursuing these plans. Bulldog's questions were timely, needed and important. With others in attendance it was particularly useful. These actions clearly outlined what would be expected of the participants. The president's presence and remarks underlined the significance and support of this initiative.

Grim: The expectations regarding the roles and responsibilities of the superintendents and general supervisors regarding project selection, coaching and support were not as clearly defined. This would prove to be a significant deficiency later in the process.

To Be Determined: Bulldog became the spokesperson for the group in this meeting. Because of his confident nature and extensive experience, he dared to insist that gains be tangible and measurable. The others, who were silent and appeared more passive, may have accepted lesser expectations.

Observations: Although not in perfect conformance to Best Practice Four—crystallizing expectations—the actions at Ovation were above average for a first time effort such as this.

- This president used his leverage and communications skills to ensure the training would be successful—beyond knowledge and test scores and even beyond application and project achievement—to developing the participants' pride, self-esteem, and motivation.

  Follow the Ovation Story as it continues in the following chapters.

Application of Best Practice Four

The most significant ideas for me in this chapter were:

_____

As a result, I intend to:

_____

Action Prompt:

- Take time to chat with a few people in the production, processing or customer service areas and casually ask, "What's giving you folks the most headaches these days?" Their answers indicate possible areas for improvement. Ask how often this occurs and you gain an insight into the frequency and severity of the problem and therefore the extent of the opportunity for improvement.

- Summarize what you learned as a result of these encounters below: _____

- Are expectations established in your organization for participants, their direct managers and the trainer/facilitator prior to or during training? **Circle one of the following:** Yes   No   Unsure

- Before or during training events, are application projects selected by each participant or with their direct manager? **Circle one of the following:** Yes   No   Unsure

- What do you think should happen?

_____

The next chapter focuses on the need to monitor progress, mentor and coach.

Chapter 7

Best Practice Five

Launch Initiatives with Dynamic Leadership and Take Positive Action to Ensure Success

Reason: Doing this demonstrates interest, importance
and ensures prompt intervention if required.

INSPIRE

Leaders relentlessly upgrade their team,
using every encounter as an opportunity to
evaluate, coach and build self-confidence.

–Jack Welch in *Winning*

Best Practice Five
Launch training initiatives with dynamic leadership then monitor progress and take positive action to ensure success.

Once the Leadership Development Team (LDT) determines the purpose, desired outcomes, the scope and nature of the training initiative, it is important to launch it with enthusiasm and dynamic leadership. With this, you present the depth and breadth of the training plus the expectations for the group. Then it is essential to monitor progress and take positive action to ensure success.

The Details: Whenever possible, have the Unit Leader launch each training initiative. This visibly demonstrates the leader's support, interest and importance both to the participants and to the organization. Once expectations are eroded by a leader's neglect, future expectations are not taken seriously. Eventually they are ignored totally. Such expectations then become meaningless, until a new leader is appointed, and that person in turn is tested.

At the launch of a training initiative, the Unit Leader is encouraged to outline the purpose and parameters of the training. As importantly, the leader is encouraged to share his or her mission, vision, values and high expectations. The following are some of the essentials to be covered.

The Unit Leader:

1. Explains how and why this initiative is significant to the achievement of corporate strategies and to the participants.

2. Challenges the participants "to be and do their best" explaining the reason this training has been selected, why it is scheduled at this time and for these particular people.

3. Challenges them to maximize their learning and apply the skills on the job, and to gain both valuable personal knowledge and skills.

4. Communicates how progress will be measured and reported and how results will be evaluated. Mentions that

improvements should appear on regular reports that are a normal part of the organization's operations.

5. Schedules regular reporting meetings to monitor training progress and ensure prompt, appropriate corrective action as needed.

6. Commits to attending the final session to hear the results and presentations. Doing so further enhances the perceived value of the training and increases participant motivation.

Inevitably there are bumps, glitches and setbacks of one kind or another; some are minor, others are major. It is important that the LDT and the leaders involved refuse to erode the expectations or reduce the requirements. Instead, it is essential to take the necessary action to ensure progress and successful outcomes.

The first step is to determine the problem: Is it a learning difficulty or is it a behavior problem? The solution may simply involve offering a one-on-one coaching session by the facilitator or by the applicable manager for those who require extra assistance. In the few extreme cases, where the person deliberately chooses to avoid participation, or application, corrective counseling might be required. Or, if ultimately necessary, assist the individual to make a career change. Of course, HR and the participant's manager should determine if this is only evident in the training sessions or is similar behavior affecting work performance.

Have the courage to remove those who consciously and deliberately withhold their efforts or hamper the efforts of others. Such action sends an important message that these expectations are serious and non-negotiable. Provide manager coaching, facilitator assistance, or added sessions to ensure success. Similarly, if additional resources and funding are needed, ensure they are provided promptly.

Leading by Word and Deed: Some essential elements for a Unit Leader to integrate into launching the training initiative include:

- An extremely effective method for developing the management team is leading them through a review and by asking the significant questions. This is training and learning by example.

- Effective and productive training must equip participants with specific knowledge and skills (including words and phrases) that are effective and applicable to the actual challenges and situations they face on a day-to-day basis.

- If basic training doesn't generate the results required, it may be that more intensity, more in-depth, more modeling, more coaching or another facilitator is needed.

- Do not give up on the goal, make the effort required to ensure success.

- Changing behaviors and achieving higher levels of performance are most successful when the Unit Leaders, the trainer(s) and participants are all involved and participate until the goal is achieved.

- Some involvement by the Unit Leader in the facilitation/ coaching role usually generates interest, attention and respect.

The Benefits

There are great benefits to both leaders and members of the LDT to be involved (enthusiastically) with the launch. For each key player, these include:

For the Unit Leader: Provides an opportunity to communicate directly to groups and to promote their vision, values and goals. They promote understanding of the organization's challenges and strategies and invite participants to grow and contribute to the efforts. In this way leaders influence and motivate those in attendance. Often, their words are remembered long after the event.

For Line Managers: The leader's influence and inspiring words have a positive effect on the participants. Wise line managers use the opportunity to support and build on the initiative. This creates two necessary components to success: common purpose and team spirit—with respect for both.

For the HR Manager: The benefits are much the same as for the line manager with one major added benefit. The Unit Leader's attendance and words make this initiative an organizational project and not simply an HR program. A significant distinction and important perception shift. Some managers and their people undervalue HR initiatives but appreciate and support organizational efforts, particularly when communicated by the Unit Leader personally.

For the Facilitator/Trainer: Those benefits that accrue to the HR person and line managers also apply to the facilitator/trainer. Being visible at the launch as well as being a member of the LDT, provides immediate influence in the organization and enhances the facilitator's image and the responsibility of the position. It also creates a receptive mindset with the participants.

Observations: Simply approving the budget or making people available does not encourage the individual to absorb as much as they can from the course.

Ovation's Story Continues: Expectations, Launch and Execution

In the previous chapter, we saw how at Ovation the expectations for the training initiative were established at a management overview session, which the president attended. The company had formed the LDT team, prioritized their needs, then evaluated and selected the trainer/facilitators.

At this point, seven groups of participants from five plants were scheduled into the training sessions to accommodate Ovation's three-shift operations. Participating supervisors were in their usual departments for the first two hours of their shift, then at the training session for three then back in their departments for the final three hours. As the president could not be available to launch each group, one of the plant managers was assigned where needed with varying degrees of competence and effect.

Time limits and space availability impacted the progress of each group. Yet, Barbara Bradley, Plant Manager of the largest of the five plants with almost 500 employees, modeled incredible leadership behaviors that were reflected in results that had the best possible gains.

Every leader's reputation is created one day and one incident at a time over many years. Barbara's was built the same way. In describing her, others would say she was a straight shooter, determined, practical and reliable. The V.P. of manufacturing who mentored her rise through the ranks from plant employee to plant manager early on had identified her leadership characteristics.

While some managers complained of the effort required to make their supervisors available and the disruption to their normal routine, Barb met with her supervisors, announced the training, explained the expected results, and praised the company initiative. Then she took two more steps. She told them that she believed they would perform well in the sessions and she was certain that they would be the best. Barb confided, "One of the important elements here is to select projects that will not only produce great results, but that will make our jobs easier and our departments more efficient. Walk through your departments, be alert for actions, situations, and other issues that you have wished you had time to do something about." She continued, "If you need advice, or help, or just want to discuss ideas, let's talk."

Within days, two of her supervisors approached Barb with a bag of work gloves saying, "We think we've found a project. As you suggested, we've been keeping our eyes open and noticed that many of our people are changing their gloves three or four times a day. Employees pick up a clean pair when they arrive and throw them into the trash barrel when they go to lunch and then pick up a clean pair again before going back to their jobs. It's the same story at the afternoon break and then they toss the gloves out when they leave for the day."

Barb enthused, "What a fantastic opportunity. What have you done so far?"

They responded with, "We've learned that there are five types of gloves in use. The cheapest is a cotton glove and the most expensive is a special heat resistant glove but we don't know the actual cost. Would you check with purchasing to find out the cost?"

"Consider it done," Barb replied. "Keep in mind that you will be doing a presentation at the final session, so keep all of your information," she added. Then she continued with, "What's your next step?"

The supervisors replied, "Next, we are going to estimate the weekly usage, and calculate the total weekly cost. Then we thought we would put up a display of the gloves and prices. After that we will circulate and ask people to change gloves less often and also ask for other suggestions they have."

"Sounds doable," she said, "I will get back to you with the prices. In the meantime check with the supplies crib to see what usage records they have." As she walked away she said a quiet, "Yes!" She knew this could be a goldmine project.

The cost of the high volume cotton glove manufactured overseas was less than $2.00 per pair. At the other end of the scale, the heat resistant glove, made domestically was almost $14.00 per pair. An average of 60 employees used gloves. The frequency of changes resulted in usage of 180 gloves per day, 900 per week in the two departments.

By the end of the following week, the display board was up and the purpose explained to employees. At the end of seven days the supervisors reported usage down by 63%. An added benefit came from one employee who suggested that the dirty cotton gloves be sent out for washing and then re-use. Another suggested contacting the heat resistant glove manufacturer for methods of extending the life of their gloves. Both were implemented two weeks prior to the course conclusion. Once all ideas were fully implemented usage had declined by 93%.

Aware that the president, plant managers and superintendents would be at the final session, Barb coached each of her supervisors on how to present their information effectively. Then she asked the facilitators to schedule a special session on presentation skills to develop their skills and confidence. While participants were obviously nervous, they were "prepared, pumped and proud."

In her training session, Barb emphasized that in presenting information to management it is important to be factual. Show whether figures were actual or estimated. Finally, she suggested they use annualized figures, explaining that budgets and operating reports were compiled on this basis. "It makes the numbers even more impressive," she emphasized. Barb's dynamic duo reported annualized project savings of $62,387 at the final session. While some of the ideas had not yet been fully implemented, they were mentioned and the savings were estimated at an additional $22,000. The cost of washing the gloves was deducted from the total savings.

Some savings were difficult to estimate—such as the fact that lower usage would result in less work in the supplies crib, fewer purchase orders to issue and fewer invoices to process. These savings were not included or even estimated but simply considered an extra benefit.

Observations: Many opportunities for improvements and savings exist openly, within eyesight, but the conditions and practices have existed for so long they are considered normal. Training can and should be used as a catalyst to garner these savings.

- Without Barb's involvement, the cost figures they needed may not have been provided. They may have been told they were, "confidential." On the other hand, the fact that these numbers were shared created a feeling of mutual trust.

- Results in other areas varied and generally reflected the degree of Unit Leader support. It is unacceptable and unconscionable that managers or other so-called leaders fail to endorse and assist their people in such efforts. By their lack of action, they erode or eliminate possible gains. Usually, without realizing it, they also undermine the respect, loyalty and motivation of their employees.

Ovation's Progress Report

(Progress is rated in terms of Grim, Good, Great or To Be Determined)

Great: Barb was outstanding in launching the efforts in her plant and in coaching her participating supervisors. Consequently, two of them achieved excellent results. This was a major contribution to the company.

All were impressed with the scores achieved on the written tests. In fact one third of participants scored 100 and the balance all were 95 or above.

Good and Grim: Some leaders were not nearly as diligent as Barb. In fact several had only limited successes and a few could have/should have, been accused of negligence for their lack of support.

There was an obvious lack of coaching, mentoring and oversight by most superintendents and three of the plant managers: A challenge for the president and a possible root cause for a multitude of problems.

Finally: The LDT was satisfied and in fact surprised by the results achieved. They hadn't experienced these kinds of results from training before; therefore, the measurable gains were considered a bonus.

It was obvious that in spite of the introductory management meeting and the urgings of the president, there was a disconnect between the executive/management group and the first-line supervisor/participants. This gap eroded the results achieved.

Close monitoring is necessary in the early stages to ensure that every participant has selected or been assigned a meaningful project. (In some cases it is preferable to have the participants suggest one or more project areas and discuss the potential gains.)

In addition to all other gains, the president learned a great deal about the capability and commitment of each plant manager, the superintendents and more about each supervisor their confidence and presentation ability. This was as valuable as the monthly performance statistics.

The Ovation story continues in the next chapter

Observations: While a degree of uniformity of training within a multi-unit organization may be desirable, there are exceptions. Head office personnel need to ensure remote locations receive training that is most important to their local needs and to achieve their outcomes rather than meet an arbitrary head office mandate.

Giving participants details about the importance of the training and their participation is necessary at the launch. Remember that participants rarely rave about completing a course that is simple and easy. In fact they often complain that it was a waste of time. However, they long remember a course where they had to make a maximum effort and were successful.

Application of These Ideas

For me personally, the most significant ideas in this chapter were:

_____

As a result, I intend to:_____

> Reason: It's motivational on many levels building pride, team spirit and a can-do, have-done positive attitude.

Action Prompt:

- In your opinion, how diligent are managers in mentoring participants during and after participation in training programs?

   Circle one: Usually   Seldom   Never   Uncertain

   Enter your intended action(s) in your daily planner or computer scheduler.

> *In the next chapter we discover the power of celebration and learn how to make it a generator of team spirit, self-esteem and pride.*

Chapter 8

Best Practice Six

Celebrate Achievements then Record and Report the Gains

INSPIRE

Like rewards and recognition, training motivates people by showing them a way to grow, that the company cares, and that they have a future.

–Jack Welch in Winning

Best Practice Six

Celebrate enthusiastically and affirm achievements
then record and report the gains.

This chapter addresses both elements, first the celebration event and then the debriefing meeting.

Researchers have reported that leaders at all levels too often fail to praise efforts and outstanding results. This chronic lack of motivational influence often applies to training outcomes as well. By its very nature praise motivates the participants to own the gains and continue the success.

Jack Welch author of *Winning* expresses his disappointment in the lack of celebrating achievements in this way, "I harped on the importance of celebrating for twenty years. But during may last trip as CEO to our training centre in Crotonville, I asked the hundred or so managers in the class, 'Do you celebrate enough in your units?' Even knowing what I wanted them to say, less than half answered yes."

Too often when training ends, an inexpensive, computer generated certificate is handed out and the facilitator says, "That's it, we are out of here," and everyone simply leaves. A dismal fizzling completion to what could have been a dynamite event.

Paul Anka, singer and songwriter once said, "Good is the enemy of great."

We would go further and say, "Good is often a barrier to better and best." This can be a time of excitement, inspiration, and celebration. It's also an ideal opportunity for the leaders to again share their vision, acknowledge the achievements and express confidence in the ability of their people.

The Celebration—A Guideline

Make the final session a memorable event. A few ideas to make this a reality are:

1. Develop numerous awards and mention these awards at every session. These may include:

   - Those who best applied the methods and achieved the greatest tangible results. (Three to five people.)

- Those who not only used the course methods but encouraged others to apply them.
  (Nominated and voted by the participants themselves.)

- Those who made serious effort but the results may have been either disappointing or may require additional time to become a reality.

2. Have each participant make a brief (2 to 4 minute presentation) on how they used an element of the course content and the results they achieved. Such presentations always impress the management team. Participants may be apprehensive, but with some preparation during the course, they surprise themselves at their own ability, and it generates lasting confidence. For example, Barbara the plant manager at Ovation was so impressed by the presentations her supervisors made, that she now has each do a brief presentation at their monthly production meetings.

3. Have the Unit Leader speak to the group. The result should be that the participants feel valued, that their efforts and results are appreciated and see themselves to be winners and important to the organization's continued success.

   - Thank everyone for their efforts including the participants, the facilitator, HR personnel, line managers and anyone else who may have coached the participants. Be generous, genuine and effusive with praise.

   - Present impressive completion certificates to each person, who has earned it, and shake their hand.

   - Ask a person with camera skills to take a picture of each presentation and of the group. Ensure each participant receives a copy.

   - Inspire and motivate by reminding them of the vision, values and goals, and that they and the organization are at their best and when customers get the best products and services they are capable of providing.

4. Finally, the leader reminds everyone that their organization is in a competitive market and by using their new skills and knowledge they will increase the likelihood of continued success for all.

Beware of a possible "Grinch"

There may be some manager who finds excuses as to why, "it can't be done."

- They would erode the enjoyment of an ice-cream sundae by eliminating the cherry on top.

- They would remove candles from birthday cakes and omit ribbons from gifts.

- They would do away with all celebration and the joy of achievement.

- Share with this person the benefits, which could accrue and recruit them for active participation in the process.

Authors of the book *In Search of Excellence*, report that at Tupperware the president and his senior managers participated for 30 days a year in Jubilees, aimed at feting the success of their 15,000 salespersons and managers. They go on to say that similar celebrations were held at a wide range of high tech and other companies. Obviously, they do it, because it's motivational for all, it pays and they enjoy it. The next anecdote is an example of what can be—the possible and the potential.

A Race for the President's Cup: A major life insurance company encourages and celebrates success by scheduling an annual President's Challenge. During this 30-day period everyone is urged to sell and process every possible policy. Each person goes all out to maximize his or her efforts. At the conclusion there is an impressive banquet with numerous awards, which are presented by the president. Every award winner and their partner are photographed with the president.

The event dominates the company newsletter both in the run-up to the campaign and afterwards. The winners also earn a place for their photograph on the company's Wall of Fame, which is located on both sides of the corridor leading to the president's office. It motivates the sales force, generates excitement and enthusiasm, and at the same time demonstrates what is possible. The payoff to all concerned? Priceless!

Ovation Automotive: *Their Celebration*

In the previous chapter, we saw how Ovation learned the importance of an enthusiastic launch and consistent coaching. Prior to the celebration itself, participants had already achieved a significant gain in that they were able to apply the knowledge and skills they learned. They felt that special power and confidence that is realized when something learned is used, and the results are recognized by themselves and others.

There was also a feeling of special recognition because the president and plant managers attended. The fact that these senior management people led the applause after each presentation was the 'icing on the cake.' Employees and supervisors rarely have an opportunity to hear the president or CEO speak. Such events create a feeling of team spirit, of being in on things, and valued. This is always important but possibly more so for first line and second line supervisors who at times feel they are in a forgotten land between the plant employees and executives.

President Tom Garrison, knew that what he said and how he said it would be discussed by many during the next few days and remembered by some for much longer. Tom began by lavishly praising the participants for their efforts. His praise extended to those superintendents and plant managers who had worked with and helped their supervisors in the selection of projects and the gains achieved. Tom made it a point to say, "We have a challenge in the future to generate more of this type of support."

Obviously Tom was an experienced hand at this. He knew how to engage and relate to his audience. He didn't "sugar coat" his message. Instead he said, "We are in a fierce battle as a company and we are the company. As suppliers to the automotive manufacturers we are always being pressured for price reductions because they have to compete with offshore producers. When we cut waste, we cut unnecessary cost. This allows us to do one or more things such as trim our prices, to be more competitive and gain additional business. Or, we can use some of the savings to invest in research and new equipment, and by the way it also means we can do more training and have funds available for future wage and salary increases. Or we could finally add something to our bottom-line profits, which would help the price of our stock and make the stockholders happy. Any one or all of these end up making our jobs and future more secure."

"How can I communicate the importance of such savings better than using this glove project as an example," he said. "To gain the equivalent of the $80,000 in profit we would have to raise prices by about 5%, which is virtually impossible in this business. Or we would have to increase sales by 15% at current prices to achieve the same gain. The sales people would tell you how difficult that would be."

Tom concluded with, "I am immensely proud and pleased with your accomplishments and it is a pleasure and an honor for me to be here and to present each of you with your completion certificate."

> **What the president didn't mention was that the savings on this single project covered most of the training cost for all of the participants: the total effort, including the cost of the facilitator's fees, course materials and the celebration.**

The Post-Training Debriefing Meeting

While a celebration in and of itself is a powerful motivating factor, the follow-up process of recording, reporting and debriefing offers a host of added benefits. In a nutshell, a celebration is *participant* focused while the debriefing is *process* focused. The team assesses what has been achieved and what requires development. Unfortunately, too few organizations use this technique to extract the knowledge gained from the training experience. The reasons are many and include:

- It hasn't been done before; therefore no one expects or plans for it.

- No one realizes the value of potential benefits.

- Those involved are uncertain about how to organize this type of meeting.

- They are concerned about potential difficulties or possible negative repercussions.

- It's easier, less work and safer to do nothing.

As a result, an opportunity for additional gain is lost. To enable you to pursue these possibilities the following guideline is provided.

A Guideline for Conducting the Post-Training Debriefing Meeting

The Agenda: It is usually most useful when The Seven Best Practices are listed as the topics for the meeting. The final item should be scheduling the next LDT meeting and defining its purpose.

The Chairperson: Is usually the HR leader who prepares the agenda and ensures the trainer/facilitator and others are prepared to report.

The Unit Leader: Attends and is the first and the last to speak. The Unit Leader acknowledges the efforts and results achieved. In addition, the contribution to the organization's strategies for competitive advantage and growth are mentioned. Commenting favorably on changes in behaviors he or she has noticed as well as the observed application of the course methods will encourage continuation. (It is important that the Unit Leader evaluate the presentations separating fact from fiction.)

Neither the HR leader, nor the trainer/facilitator has the authority or the leverage to ensure that other managers meet their commitments. It is left to the Unit Leader to meet one-on-one with certain managers to discuss their performance (or behavior deficiencies.)

A powerful technique used by some is to ensure that leadership behavior is a topic on every meeting agenda.

The Trainer/Facilitator (Internal or External): Reports on knowledge and skills gained, participation, behavior changes and participant reactions and application of the methods. The benefits multiply when this person also reports on suggestions made by participants regarding improvements required in day-to-day operations. Spontaneous discoveries unearthed during the sessions are valuable and need to be pursued. The Unit Leader must delegate that responsibility to a member of the team. Finally, at this point the trainer should share hindrances to be eliminated, suggested process changes to be made, and potential next steps to improve and continue the process.

When an external trainer/facilitator is used it is important to consider this person an integral and significant member of the LDT. This person brings unique insights and experiences gained in a variety of organizations, which can be value-added to your organization. However, this is only possible if they are privy to the desired outcomes established by the LDT and have access to the members individually to discuss and clarify the expectations. These contacts also provide an opportunity for the person to share methods and techniques that have proven effective elsewhere and could be appropriate and valuable here. Whether the facilitator is internal or external, this person needs to have a common understanding with the LDT members regarding the importance of achieving the challenging expectations and providing the required resources and coaching.

Operational Line Manager(s): Report regarding on-the-job behavior changes, application and measurable results achieved. They share how they personally have lead by example and coached their participants in the use of the methods—and their plans to achieve sustainability. Some may be embarrassed by their lack of application, results and mentoring efforts. The Unit Leader should make it a point to ask each one, "What are you going to do differently next time?" His second question, "Do you know now where areas exist that need to be improved, and can I count on you to begin making those changes?" Finally he should ask each, "Do you need assistance from me, our HR manager or the external facilitator?"

HR Leader: Highlights the positive behavior changes attributed to the training and points out particular areas for future emphasis. This person develops a "This Time List" of what went well and a "Next Time List" of changes and improvements for the next initiative. Suggestions and needs for the next phase are accumulated and presented. This step acts as a reminder for the team of the next meeting when future needs will again be prioritized.

The Team: As a group, the team develops an action plan to ensure continued application of the knowledge, skills and behaviors in order to ensure they become automatic habits, sustainable as they contribute to creating a new culture.

Tips for Optimal Debriefing Meetings:

- When determining measurable gains they must be realistic, reasonable and efficient. Keep your time limits for this task realistic. Training personnel at one major banking institution say they devote three days to recording results for each day of training completed. This seems to be excessive, inefficient, and unnecessary.

- Use existing operational reports to indicate results wherever possible. It adds to credibility.

- In some situations "guesstimates" by a group of experienced people are as valuable as more detailed examinations. Keep it simple—calculating to two or three decimal places does not indicate greater accuracy or validity.

- Avoid the trap of undervaluing gains. This undermines the feeling of achievement and motivation. It may occur, in cases where the results are not immediately measurable or if they may not be implemented during the current budget year.

- Keep presentations brief. Ask presenters to use a list of key points to stay on track.

- Use the same report format for all participants. Include areas for focus such as "opportunity," "action taken," "results achieved," both *tangible* and *intangible*.

- A few managers through their disinterest, lack of effort and negative interaction erode the effort and motivation of their people and in turn the employees who report to them. Don't allow such people to pull you all down—rise above and emphasize success and results.

- Keep these meetings positive and focused on what has been and is being achieved. It's not a time for problem solving.

- Avoid singling out individual managers for negative feedback. The Unit Leader on a personal basis should take such corrective steps promptly.

- Ensure all understand that the ultimate purpose of training is not the training itself but the capability developed, the continued application and the results achieved.

Ovation Automotive: The Debriefing to Report Results

The LDT members were assembled in a conference room adjacent to the president's office. Those present included all who attended the pre-course launch, Tom Garrison, the president, Tony the manager of training, the manager of continuous improvement and ourselves, the facilitators.

Tom began with, "First, I want to acknowledge and thank Tony for his efforts. As training manager, he has been the person who has coordinated these efforts, the scheduling, and the interface with our facilitators. I particularly appreciate the fact that he didn't let his ego get in the way of selecting an outside training source rather than attempting to do this himself. Internal and external resources should always be considered. Obviously both have certain advantages depending on the circumstances, content, and trainer expertise. It is imperative that from time to time we open ourselves to new methods, ideas and viewpoints from outside the company and then put them to use in growing our own capability."

He proceeded by asking, "Tony as training manager, what do you feel were the most important elements of these efforts?"

Tony responded, "This may surprise some, but I think having your involvement during the planning at the beginning, at the final presentations and now at this debriefing are what I appreciate most. It resulted in everyone working together for common objectives and in full agreement on such areas as the expectations. Without this direct face-to-face input it would have been difficult to achieve this focus with e-mails or verbally communicated through other people. In addition, it demonstrated to everyone that you were fully behind this initiative and expected us all to support it and to achieve the results. These items would be at the top of my list. Next is the professionalism of the trainer/facilitators who knew not only the content and methods but how to respond in positive ways to negative issues. I was able to learn a great deal from working with them during every step. My third element would be the projects and measurable results, these truly got most participants involved and in such a way that they felt was productive and useful."

Others at the table agreed on the value and importance of holding the pre-course planning meeting to discuss the purpose of the training and developing clear-cut expectations. They added that the presentation for the plant managers and superintendents to brief them on content, methods, and scheduling gained their support. In addition, the involvement of managers and supervisors from other departments promoted co-operation and common understanding and use of similar methods.

Next, Tom asked for our viewpoint. We agreed that all of the elements mentioned were important. Omitting any one of them would have lessened the efforts and results. "One thing that was vital, which we need to add to the list, is the importance of remaining firm regarding the expectations. Once expectations are ignored, by-passed or reduced, they quickly become meaningless not only for the current activity but will erode their power for future efforts. To your credit, you all held firm on them," we continued, "and as you know they were met by all of the participants."

At this point, Tom interjected saying, "There are a few more points we should add to our 'This Time' list.

- **First** is that expectations were exceeded and significant payback was generated.

- **Second** is that we know that learning took place. Further some of this knowledge will be retained and applied for years to come.

- **Third**, and similarly, some of the savings generated will continue for another year, some for several years, a valuable cumulative effect that is too often overlooked."

Tom continued, "From my point of view, another benefit was seeing our people make their presentations. Frankly, I was impressed as much by their skill and self-confidence as I was by the descriptions of the projects and the numbers generated. This made me realize again what talented and committed people we have as a resource. Let's have these folks do periodic presentations at relevant meetings and be certain that I can attend," he concluded. His enthusiasm was obvious and contagious.

Tony said, "There is another item that was useful and has almost been forgotten. A couple of weeks into the course, the facilitators met with me and informed me that participants were asking many labor relations related questions. They suggested we modify the schedule to add a one-hour question & answer segment to be conducted by Roy, our labor relations manager. That was done and resulted in positive feedback. Participants have remarked many times that both the course content and methods were practical and relevant to what they actually had to do. Let's add to our list the ideas of both being flexible and adding internal people when needed."

Now Tom turned the spotlight on us as the outside facilitators by asking, "What feedback do you have for us? What observations and suggestions should we add to our 'Next Time' list?"

We replied, "The good news is that the company has achieved measurable results estimated at about a 150% return on investment during this fiscal year. With the improvements we are suggesting, there should be even greater payback in the future. However, there are two major areas for potential improvement."

We continued, "First is the selection and support of potential projects. It was obvious that while many projects were significant, there were others that were sadly lacking and a few participants had no projects at all. They said their managers claimed that they didn't have the time to help them. That's not being critical. It's being frank. It is also a fact that in many organizations, people are totally focused on day-to-day activities and daily results. They see no reason to search for improvements. A few consider it outside their normal duties. Some actually believe that improvements are impossible. The whole prospect of continuous improvement is viewed negatively. Finally, to implement some of the changes required for improvement could be difficult for them due to approvals required and budgetary constraints, and so forth. Because achieving projects is not part of the norm, some managers ignore the coaching and support necessary for success. If these responsibilities were identified on their performance evaluations and they were held accountable, the required behaviors would likely be achieved."

"Second is the challenge of continued application of the methods. Bulldog, at the initial planning meeting, questioned whether participants would apply what they learned. This was accomplished in part because of the length of the course and the achievement of projects. Continuing such application beyond the course end requires new habits. Such habits usually become automatic after four to six weeks of repetition." At this point, it was decided that their next meeting would be about continuity.

"Let's move on to the specific gains that were achieved," the president suggested. During the next half hour, team members presented reports detailing the following actual gains by type of gain.

Once Only gains: There were several in the maintenance and quality departments.

Continuing gains: included the glove usage project. (This could also be termed a "spontaneous discovery.")

Cascading Gains: were achieved in two of the plants where scrap was reduced.

Propagation of gains: was again the usage of gloves, which was expanded to all departments in all five plants and yielded significant on-going savings.

Another Spontaneous Discovery: was that Bulldog had instructed his superintendents to review the past month's operating report in detail and account for any expenses exceeding the budgeted amount. After some had begun this onerous and arduous task, a wiser person suggested, "We can't change what's done, why don't we see if we can do this on a daily basis, while it is happening and take immediate action?" They did and many costs were avoided.

Ovation's Progress Report
(Progress is rated in terms of Grim, Good, Great or To Be Determined)

Great: Participants learned the incredible annualized cost of everyday items and how easily they are wasted and how quickly the costs mount.

Supervisors who had significant projects felt a true sense of achievement not only because of the savings but also in their own ability to assemble and present the information.

The celebration was a source of conversations, pride and team spirit.

Holding the debriefing captured the extent of the gains, and highlighted what had been most effective and identified steps for future improvement.

Good: Financial information and assistance for those who needed data was beneficial.

Grim: The two most pathetic comments heard from a few participants in the course were, "We couldn't find a project to work on." (As a result we now provide thought starter lists to our clients to reference) and the second was, "My manager said, 'don't bother me, go find a project yourself.'"

To Be Determined: The team and its members expressed positive intentions and made the expected commitments. But would they continue to move forward?

Those few plant managers and superintendents who made little or no effort to support their people and this initiative, by their very nature are likely to continue such behavior. It will require due diligence and one-on-one dialogue by the president to ensure behavior change with these managers.

Observations: Most organizations have employees ready and willing to tackle existing problems but either the leaders don't know how to initiate action, which is a training need, or they lack the initiative, which is a performance deficiency to be addressed.

By their lack of support, some of these middle managers unintentionally de-motivated their supervisors. They could have used the training as an opportunity to work with them and so build loyalty, respect and team spirit.

Application of These Ideas

The most significant ideas in this chapter for me were:

_____

As a result, I intend to:

_____

Action Prompt:

- Enter what you know needs to happen in your organization and the potential benefits in your computer scheduler and then initiate some action within five days.

  In the next chapter, we learn the keys to achieving culture change, continuous improvement and sustainability.

Chapter 9

Best Practice Seven

Refine and Repeat the Process

Reason: It improves the process and promotes continuation
of the best practices in all areas affected.

A mind that has been stretched will never
return to its original dimension.

–Albert Einstein

Best Practice Seven

Refine and repeat the process to achieve
competitive advantage, culture
change and sustainability.

The seventh and final best practice is devoted to sustaining the gains and changes until they become an integral part of the organization's culture. This means all of the elements of the previous six best practices— from using training as a change agent to achieving continued competitive advantage. It means the ongoing use of a Leadership Development Team to prioritize the needs, to ensure training and facilitation excellence, to prompt the application of the knowledge and skills developed, to celebrate these positive activities and schedule regular debriefing by the LDT to continue to refine the process.

Doing this ensures the establishment of a learning, growing, evolving and competitive workplace; an organization with people who are able and eager to seize the opportunities presented by never-ending change. Most employees relish learning, enjoy challenges and make real connections with others who thrive in the same dynamic atmosphere.

In many organizations, managers and leaders strive to achieve this highly desirable state. The sad fact is that too many fall far short. A few never attempt it, feeling that technology or other methods will generate faster, more certain results. Why is this the case?

First, it begins with how "training" has been perceived. The crux of the sustainability challenge is that training has long been regarded as an educational event or a course or a program rather than a never-ending development process. Traditionally, training has been planned for certain dates in a calendar and perceived as complete when the day is done. Therefore, the Unit Leader or line managers delegate the efforts downwards with little if any direct involvement. Since executives and managers don't seem to be involved, the function is seen as "nice to do" rather than a necessity. Too many employees, supervisors and managers therefore view it as unimportant. Nor is anyone in authority tasked with ensuring application. Going further, no one monitors the activities to determine what has been achieved. The results often are considered satisfactory as long as participants say they enjoyed it. What this does is create a belief system within the organization where "expectations" for the training are minimal. Unfortunately, when little is expected, little is gained.

Refining and repeating the process for continued gains is greatly influenced by the organization's Unit Leader who may hold the title CEO, president, plant manager or other. If this leader believes that training can and will contribute to the organization's performance, he or she will ensure that it gets done. This key belief is strongest when the Unit Leader has personally experienced the positive outcomes of training and its contribution to profits and growth.

For those who have the initiative, desire, and commitment to achieve sustainability, our advice is to follow the steps outlined below and in the next chapter. If your Unit Leader has not experienced successful training efforts, keep in mind that their spoken or unspoken challenge is "show me." Therefore, choose an opportunity that will have the greatest support of others, greatest likelihood of success and utilize the expertise of the best resources available. Build a base of success one step at a time to ensure enduring support. As this is being done, keep a longer-term perspective in mind as well. Think beyond the here and now and plan for future changes and challenges.

It is essential that when there is a change in senior management that the new leader(s) be informed of past successes of the training efforts and their measurable contributions to performance. Then communicate the forward plans and priorities already in place and the reasons for these choices and obtain buy-in. It is important to also share their participatory role in the leadership of these efforts and those of the LDT. We've found that frequent changes in Unit Leaders or managers erode continuity of purpose, resolve and support unless the bridging communication described above takes place.

Essential to ensuring sustainability is to identify training as an important method of ensuring future improvements. This means defining training as the catalyst and channel for the continuing pursuit of the competitive advantage. Here are some suggestions for how to get this done:

- At Ovation they fostered this initiative by holding debriefing meetings, where they developed and utilized "This Time," and "Next Time" lists and did so on a regular basis.

- Make training and development more than a single event; make it a key element in the ongoing process for continuous improvement.

- The Unit Leader must regularly and consciously prompt leaders to follow the seven best practices which constitute the process, set new priorities, and inculcate the initiative into the organization's financial, human resource and other management systems with regular progress reporting and accountability.

- As new people are promoted or recruited from outside to leadership positions, they need to be oriented into this aspect of their leadership responsibility. They need to know about the LDT, the utilization of training as a resource for organizational goals achievement and past contributions to performance. Finally, each of these people must understand their roles and responsibilities as active, involved leaders.

- This requires discipline to avoid distractions, overcome obstacles and to remain on course despite other concerns and issues. It requires relentless pursuit.

Increasingly, we are being asked about these issues of culture change, continuous improvement and sustainability. The questions usually end with, "Can you people do this for us?" The answer is always the same as when we are asked if we can change attitudes or if we can increase sales revenues, gross margin and profitability.

The answer is, "No we cannot do that for you, but we can usually do it with you in a partnership. In addition, we will show you how to do this so that you can do it yourselves in future."

The anecdotes that follow, illustrate situations that facilitate these aspects and those key management attitudes that preclude successful achievement. The next story indicates that **this** company, with **this** management at **this** time is not a likely candidate for continuous improvement or culture change. The managers didn't feel the need to improve their methods. Their attitude was that others needed to change and they didn't. They also lacked the motivation to lead by example. So while the training was effective at creating the desired behavior change, it did not rise to the challenge of changing the culture.

Smoke Signals at Remington Tobacco

The Situation at Remington Tobacco: At this tobacco processing plant, the most frequent complaint was the ineffectiveness of meetings. Participants were frustrated and fuming about what they considered a waste of their time. Managers, in turn, complained that meetings seldom resulted in decisions or action. This might be described as meetings where—when all is said and done—much is *said* but little is *done*. Here was a situation where no one seemed to know how to conduct a productive meeting. To make it worse, ineffective managers passed on their ineffective methods and habits to others who followed their example. One of the few decisions everyone could agree on was that training on how to conduct an effective meeting was necessary. One manager went so far as to calculate the number of people attending meetings each week and the average time spent in the meetings and the approximate cost per hour.

The Solution: Approval was quickly obtained and the sessions promptly scheduled. Those attending the sessions eagerly took part and participated fully. All agreed that the content and methods were appropriate and useful. They were impressed by the trainer's skills and personality. But at the second session, a few brave souls spoke out saying, "This is great stuff, why isn't senior management participating? They are the people who chair most of the meetings and most need to change the way they conduct them."

Early on the participants learned what should be happening and realized that their managers had an obvious lack of ability. The HR manager had the unenviable task of being the messenger to carry this feedback to upper management. Reluctantly they agreed to participate, all the while claiming, "It isn't actually necessary, we know what we're doing, and it's those who attend that need to improve their participation and attitude."

The Results and Sustainability: On completion of the training, all agreed that there was a marked improvement in effectiveness. One of the factors was that any slips in conducting the meetings were now quickly noted and commented on by those in attendance. This created prompt changes in behaviors.

Will the people continue to use the knowledge and skills? Very likely, because the participants will keep reminding each other and they will remind management as well. Eventually the behaviors will become self-perpetuating. It will not however likely change the more deeply rooted problem of management being disconnected from reality. In fact, several years later this facility was closed and the jobs exported to a lower-cost country.

A Dealer Deals with Sustainability:

In day-to-day encounters with his sales people the President/Owner of an earthmoving equipment dealership on the west coast regularly tosses one or more questions at them. It might be about product specifications, or equipment application or one of the sales techniques. After every training event, regardless of duration, he makes certain that participants receive a reminder card listing the key points. These memory joggers are provided again in company newsletters. Periodically he schedules a brief competition during coffee break. His opinion is, "You can't use what you don't remember." As the owner, he believes that using the knowledge gained will increase sales and profitability.

The Results: Sales and service personnel here are considered to be among the most knowledgeable and effective in their field, an enviable reputation for the company and its capability.

This situation will, likely continue for as long as this president owns the company. Application, retention and sustainability require the on-going, demonstrated, conscious leadership of the Unit Leader. For sustainability, the "mind set" has to change from, "The course is over and back to business as usual," to the perspective of, "This event is over but application never ends." Some leaders address this by using an outside training resource and a three to five year commitment to ensure continuity and forward momentum.

At Seating Solutions Inc.

The Situation at Seating Solutions Inc.: On occasion, when a trainer/facilitator discusses a potential training initiative with the Unit Leader they question whether this leader truly wants what they say they want. In this situation, we asked ourselves, "Does this leader truly want continuous improvement?"

While conducting leadership training for Bob Patrick the plant manager and his direct reports at Seating Solutions, Bob asked, "Can you people do continuous improvement (CI) training for our team leaders and their hourly paid team members in the plant?" When assured that we could, he quickly had the purchase order prepared. Fortunately, before beginning this new assignment, HR Manager Ken Lewis suggested we join him in a tour through the plant. It turned out this was simply an excuse for a confidential conversation. Ken had a purpose in mind. He wanted to caution us about a potential problem.

"Before launching the CI Training, there is something that you should be aware of," he began quietly. "There are times when Bob, our plant manager, gets carried away and takes on more than he can handle," he said diplomatically. "About two years ago, Bob contracted with another firm to do CI training here. Six teams were formed, two for each product line. The training was done and the teams began to hold meetings. Bob promised to attend every team meeting, assuring the teams they had his full support. After attending twice, he became embroiled in other priorities and never attended again." Ken confided, "It's to the credit of the team leaders and their members that they discontinued meetings saying there was no point in continuing without management support. They could easily have continued to meet, avoiding their work in the plant, but they didn't."

The Solution: Being forewarned, the challenge was how best to proceed. The information Ken shared had to be used carefully while addressing the issue and assessing Bob's seriousness and commitment. We had to do this without divulging the source and betraying confidentiality.

At our next meeting with Bob, it was simply suggested that in preparation for the proposed training, a number of people be interviewed to determine the organization's readiness for a CI training process. With the interviews completed, we shared with Bob what we had learned about the previous effort. He readily agreed that he had been remiss, blaming the reason on the chaotic circumstances at that time. He concluded with, "What happened in the past is past and won't happen again." In spite of his emphatic assurances, there were lingering doubts. To ensure a successful launch for the process and the training, Bob was asked to personally announce the process to all employees briefly at the end of a shift and then to follow this with a talk to team leaders and members, once again pledging his support.

To his credit, Bob did speak to all of the employees, team leaders and team members. To his discredit, Bob did not participate as promised. Once again, he was a leader MIA—Missing in Action.

The Results: Bob left the company a few months later. Whether it was voluntary is still a matter of speculation. Ken Lewis, the HR manager, had the courage to warn us. His input remained confidential. He knew his boss and his behavioral patterns. Bob was a "type A" personality, inclined to frantic activity and usually creating more chaos than completion. His departure left a stain that would make it more difficult for his replacement to implement continuous improvement or any other team-based initiative.

At Community Power Inc.

The Situation at Community Power Inc.: This example illustrates the type of leadership most likely to achieve both continuous improvement and sustainability. Planned deregulation was the precipitating factor that led management to recognize that fundamental changes were going to be necessary. This public utility with nearly 400 employees, was about to be thrust from their comfortable routine as a municipal distributor of electric power and water, to an organization facing a snarling pack of eager competitors.

General Manager, Samir El-Kassim, had earned his promotions over the 22 years he had served the utility. Having progressed up through the ranks he realized that the employees and management too, had enjoyed a secure, comfortable, well-paid existence. Now as leader-in-charge, he accepted the fact that he must prepare the organization for the shock of competition and culture change.

HR Manager, Christine Elliott, called us explaining that she had been referred to us by friends in the HR association she belonged to. She deliberately avoided providing much information leaving that for our first meeting with Samir and herself.

As you might expect at a virtual monopoly, Samir was friendly, low key and easy going. With niceties concluded he paused and said, "Let's cut to the chase. Let me lay out what needs to be done. Our employees at all levels have led a sheltered life and now the situation is changing. We have to change, not only the way we see and do things but the way we think. We have to go from comfortable to competitive and do it quickly." Samir, as the Unit Leader, accepted the responsibility for preparing the organization for a rude awakening and the shock of culture change. (This factor is a positive signal not only for likely success but sustainability as well.)

"I don't want to lose the co-operative atmosphere we now have but we need to instill a do-it-now, do-it-faster, do-it-better mind-set. Bear with me," he cautioned, "while I explain some of what we've done in the past and what we need to do in future. In the past few years we've done what I refer to as, 'Smile Training.' Our training events have usually been off-site, comfortable and they concentrated on the soft-skills such as communication, motivation, team building, etc. In our evaluations, we were satisfied if participants said they enjoyed the seminar. Seldom did anything change, and of course we didn't expect it to because we didn't ask them to do anything differently."

As Samir spoke, he seemed to be talking not only to us but also communicating to Christine the changing approach and expectations that he was about to share. He continued, "Of the things we will change, possibly the most important is our expectations. First, we will define exactly what needs to be improved and why it's important."

"Instead of a mish-mash of unrelated, disconnected topics conducted randomly from time to time, we are going to schedule training regularly and focus on the behaviors of effective leadership and we are going to structure it over a three year period. This way each topic and each session will build on what has been done before, giving us a cumulative effect. In addition our people will come to realize that this isn't a flavor-of-the-month type event, but an on-going process dedicated to being the best in the marketplace."

At this point Samir paused, to ensure that he was being understood. Then he continued saying, "Another change is that instead of only the supervisors being trained, we in senior management will be the first to participate. Doing this will create a number of benefits. Others in the organization will realize immediately that changes are taking place, and that management is leading the process. Of course, since we will insist on behavior changes, the supervisors and employees will be able to observe our changed behaviors. This puts the onus on us to demonstrate on a day-to-day basis the practices we want to promote."

"Before we continue, there is one more thing I want you to know," Samir continued, "to demonstrate my commitment to this process, I will attend every session with the first group, I will do what we ask the others to do and I will say a few words at the first session for each group." With what seemed a smirk, Samir asked challengingly, "Can you and your people do this with our help?"

The Solution: Our response was just as direct, "If you spell out clearly what is expected of participants and why, we can and will give them the knowledge and skills they need. In fact, we will do it in ways that are interesting, positive and productive. But keep in mind that none of these people work for us, we don't control their paychecks and we cannot tell them what to do. If you folks tell them what needs to be done, we will help them learn how to do it. Keep in mind that only you have the leverage necessary to require them to do what is expected. Before actually launching this initiative, let's get together to define the expectations, agree on the consequences and how between the three of us we will maintain a high level of motivation through positive feedback and coaching."

"We will do more than that," Samir interrupted, "We will agree on the content and structure of the course evaluation form, so that it reflects what has actually been achieved. At the same time we will identify organizational performance indicators and set goals for improvement. I want to see some method of identifying after each session whether participants understand and are applying the methods. Finally, I want to meet and discuss progress after every second session. Starting off on the right track prevents disappointments and recriminations in future," he concluded.

Results: Three years have passed since this effort was begun and progress has been beyond expectations and is continuing. Was it the skill of our facilitators? We simply say that great training combined with active management support—generates extraordinary results.

At Boundless Industries Inc.

The Situation at Boundless Industries Inc.: The problem was by far, most obvious at the largest of their three regional plants and President, Al Evans was well aware of the issues. The five managers in charge were constantly bickering. Each blamed the others for problems. They regularly competed for limited resources. Most serious, they were ego-driven to be right rather than do what was right for the business. Having already confronted them as a group and individually with strict orders to stop these destructive behaviors without success, Al decided in desperation to use an external resource. It was time to stop the battles within and focus on battling the outside competitors. His instructions to the HR manager and our facilitator were direct and simple:

- The challenge was not to only stop the incessant infighting, but to develop a vision, a statement of values combined with a strategy and goals; and to do this in a way that they all would buy into and willingly support on an ongoing basis.

- "Consider naming the training a problem-solving course. That should make it non-threatening and define it as a learning experience," Al suggested.

- "Allow for more than normal discussion and schedule sufficient time so that they actually work on the statements together with the facilitator keeping the process on track and moving forward.

- Give the participants weekly assignments to both apply what they have learned and to prepare a position statement for the following session's topic.

- To reinforce this effort and ensure success, advise the participants that I will attend every second session to see how they are progressing.

Meet with me the day prior to brief me. By the way, just between us for now, this isn't an 8, 10, or 12 session program. It will conclude when we've achieved the purpose I've outlined. At the final meeting, have them present their output."

The Solution: It was clear that when the managers realized that no amount of delay, excuses or differences of opinion would end this effort, they increasingly took the assignments seriously. As they did that, they found common ground, useful methods, and there was greater co-operation.

The initiative was completed after 14 grueling and sometimes contentious sessions. From then on, everyone followed the same "song-sheet." All progressed smoothly for five months. Productivity was improving and problems declining. It seemed nothing could go wrong...

Unexpectedly, the corporate president announced that a new plant manager, Sandra Burdock had been appointed to head this operation. In near panic, the team met to discuss how to cope with this situation. Their concern was the possibility that the new Unit Leader would ignore or veto their vision statement. Even worse, would she impose predetermined plans of her own?

Their strategy, formulated with such intense effort and proven effective, now seemed in danger. They were well aware of the difficulty in achieving continuity and maintaining focus. Turning again to their external resource person, they developed a proactive action plan that involved presenting their vision statement and strategy along with the monthly reports of progress to the new plant manager and doing so at the first opportunity. They tasked this external person with facilitating the meeting and achieving buy-in and support from the new Unit Leader.

The Results: There was an intangible spontaneous discovery by mid-point in the process. The managers began seeing greater co-operation between their departmental employees. When they asked their people for the reason they were told, "We see you managers finally working together and we just started doing the same."

As for the new plant manager, fortunately, she was astute enough to realize that the group had developed a strategy that produced improved results. Further, he saw that they had become a truly a cohesive team and not just a group. They had unity of purpose and commitment to co-operation. Her wisdom was obvious from her periodic question, "What do you need from me to keep this ball rolling?"

The team had learned a final, possibly the most important lesson during these efforts. Achieving sustainability requires regular oversight.

This is particularly vital when there is a change in the leadership team. It requires a planned effort to induct and inform the new person and convince them of the value and effectiveness of the process. Even more challenging is enlisting their active support on an on-going basis. Here are some key sustainability points:

- Diversity of experience, opinion and talent can and should be a positive contribution to organizational success. However, diverse elements require commitment to a common purpose.

- There are times, when simple, dogged determination and perseverance are required to overcome inertia.

- Newly appointed Unit Leaders are well advised to proceed with some caution, making an effort to understand the existing situation, the present strategy, the degree of success and the people, before launching new initiatives that could be unnecessary, inappropriate and even destructive.

- If the Unit Leader finds that the organization is already pursuing a sound strategy and it is productive, it is important to reassure those involved of the continuity of purpose and his or her personal support.

- If however, the new Unit Leader is brought in to effect change, it will usually be more accepted, supported and effective if it is a modification of what is already productive. The Unit Leader will be more successful if he or she explains what changes are needed and why, and the expected outcomes and timelines. It requires a clear and simple vision that others can "see" and a "path" that they can follow with the repeated reassurance that, "We can do this by working together."

At View-Tech Inc.

The Situation at View-Tech Inc.: As Japanese automakers established assembly operations in North America, View-Tech followed along as suppliers. In fact, they accommodated their customers further by broadening the range of components they manufactured. To ensure continuing competitive advantage, View-Tech had consciously decided that employee relations were of primary importance with the objective of remaining union-free. This included looking at cross-cultural values in regards to making change and its sustainability. Many of their competitors were unionized and as a result plagued by higher costs and periodic work stoppages.

When they established their plant in Ontario, they recruited Chris Sanchez as plant manager and tasked him not only to operate a productive plant, but also to do it in an employee-friendly atmosphere. Fortunately that suited Chris's natural inclination. He prided himself on the fact that he knew not only the names of every employee but also something of their interests and families. That was relatively simple when employment was 150. However, as the plant population quickly grew to upwards of 600 and with a second location it was becoming much more difficult.

The Solution: As Chris considered the situation, he realized that somehow he needed to instill the same values and behaviors in his managers and supervisors. He wanted a sustainable culture change and was demonstrating those behaviors at every opportunity. His challenge was that he needed to do more than model the behaviors he wanted—he needed to articulate them and explain them without personalizing the issues and lecturing the leaders.

He also realized that to achieve culture shift required more than one initiative, or one event. It needed to be an on-going process over a span of several years. In formulating his plans, Chris was certain that using an external training or consulting resource was the best solution. However, a serious hurdle was the fact that his Japanese counterparts, believed all knowledge should come from within the unit. Unfortunately, a person with that experience and capability wasn't available internally. Confident in his assessment and solution, Chris proposed a pilot training project to his Japanese associates. He reminded them of the impact that outside experts (such as Deming and Juran) had decades earlier when they brought new ideas and methods to Japanese industry. Recognizing Chris's abilities and past performance, the project was approved.

Chris met with the external facilitator regularly to clarify expectations, discuss progress and share his philosophies. "What we need is to focus our training efforts on instilling basic behaviors and avoid the distractions and disruptions of annual *flavor of the year* training topics," Chris insisted.

The Results: The initial project was successful and Chris submitted a proposal for a three-year initiative, which was approved. As that effort neared completion, he requested a further three-year extension, which was again granted. Shortly after the first initiative, Chris was promoted to be president of Canadian operations. Now three years later he has been chosen to establish a new facility planned for Mississippi.

Meanwhile, his replacement in Canada has already met with the external facilitators to ensure the process continued, and builds on what has already been done.

Sustainability of the culture change has been achieved for six years and has bridged the change in leadership, a significant achievement in this era of change and chaos.

> **Values and vision provide the foundation,**
> **strategies the plan, and training the abilities.**
> **Repetition and oversight generate the culture**
> **change and the result is competitive advantage.**

The Final Segment in the Ovation Automotive Story

The Mixed Results and Sustainability: As was planned, for several years Ovation used the basic leadership course for newly appointed supervisors. Then as a follow-on course, under pressure from their corporate headquarters, an effective communications course was launched for their supervisory leaders. Results were less than hoped for and limited by three factors: 1) the materials consisted of a three inch binder (which few participants bothered to read,) 2) the trainers were former teachers and lacked actual supervisory or managerial experience and 3) a lack of focus on application and results.

More successful, was a process engineering initiative. Great results were achieved by using process engineering teams, who were trained in the methods, assigned specific areas and provided with funds and staff support for immediate implementation. In every case, the reports of improved results were forwarded to the president, his key managers, and to corporate headquarters.

A continuing obstacle to performance improvement was the understaffed human resources department. It lacked the capacity and capability to ensure continuity and oversight. The labor relations manager remained preoccupied with grievance resolution and union complaints and demands. The root cause of these problems became increasingly obvious; the company needed an improved process for selecting supervisors and managers. Training itself could not compensate for unsuitable supervisory candidates.

Tony Apostle, the training manager, felt ill-equipped and unsuited for his responsibilities and sensed that future opportunities for advancement were elsewhere. He requested and received re-assignment as a supervisor to one of the other plants. Tom Garrison, after making numerous improvements, was promoted to head European operations. Two years later, all five plants were sold to an international competitor.

These brief summaries indicate a few of the key reasons that sustainability was *not* achieved at this organization.

Ovation's Final Progress Report

(Progress is rated in terms of Grim, Good, Great or To Be Determined)

Great: Tom Garrison, the president, the manager of continuous improvement, and most of the plant managers performed effectively. Their achievements were due primarily to the steadiness of Tom's leadership skills, his vision, encouragement and support and the influence of their corporate vice president.

Good: Tony Apostle certainly made the efforts needed but unfortunately lacked the specific skills required in this situation. The organization was constantly in a fire-fighting mode and other managers were not in a position to be of help. His reassignment was likely best for both his career and the company.

Grim: The labor relations situation was a constant grinding adversarial condition. A culture of confrontation had developed and would continue until both protagonists were replaced. The lack of a competent HR director restricted progress and sustainability.

To Be Determined: The take-over by another corporate entity made continuity and sustainability questionable. It is possible that the new owners would develop the capability in HR. This could result in improving the labor relations situation and the selection process for first-line supervisors. Further gains are always possible, the question is could the new corporate people provide the required leadership actions?

Finally: This is reality in many organizations. Much churning and turmoil exists, changes continue. Can the leaders not only cope with, but also move the organization forward and ensure the gains in this situation? Then do it again and again? Yes, if they have the unique capability, suitability and that nebulous desire—the desire, and drive to lead.

Sustainability: The Challenges

The best way to achieve this is to follow the same procedures as the budgeting and cost control process. Set annual goals and requirements; determine the measurement and reporting process. Incorporate monthly reviews and hold both human resources and line managers accountable. Continue doing this until it becomes the norm and automatic. The key leaders must receive and review progress reports on a scheduled basis. Keep these reports brief, specific, and timely.

The Requirements for Achieving and Maintaining Sustainability

1. The Unit Leader must regularly communicate the need to achieve sustainability of leadership development, demonstrate personal commitment to the ongoing process and hold the management group accountable for their behaviors and for developing their people.

2. Integrate leadership development, behavior, application and results as an integral element of the human resource management process such as:

   - Job/responsibility descriptions
   - Performance reviews
   - Progression and succession planning
   - Compensation, rewards and recognition activities

   Integrate with the financial management system, and in particular:

   - Budgeting for leadership development
   - Participation in identifying opportunities and priorities
   - Reporting on potential gains and ensuring payback is pursued
   - Providing relevant information to managers and their participants
   - Identifying improvements achieved and reflecting these gains in the cost, budgeting and performance results reports

3. Schedule orientation sessions and coaching for those who are newly promoted, transferred-in or recruited into leadership positions. This includes a "continuity plan" when a significant leader—such as the Unit Leader—leaves the organization.

4. Ensure that all people involved receive the knowledge, skills, and application methods. They must realize that this process is not an option but a key organizational strategy.

5. Discuss leadership actions, challenges and success at all meetings where results of the training and development process are discussed. The following are examples of questions that may be asked:

   - Are leaders demonstrating positive leadership behaviors? (Specifically what, when and how?)

- Are leaders regularly coaching and correcting their people on a personal basis?

- Are leaders supporting the Seven Best Practices and achieving the predetermined results?

6. Ensure information is available and utilized to inform the LDT of the priorities of the organization and the training and coaching and development needs of individuals in their various departments.

7. Monitor use of the Seven Best Practices process regularly to ensure refinement and results. (Inevitably there are a few leaders who will begin to erode or discontinue certain tools and activities believing that they are unimportant or unpleasant and will not be effective.)

8. The key leaders must demonstrate interest, vigilance and oversee the process forever. The same as is done with the monthly, quarterly and annual operating reports and performance numbers.

9. When results are not meeting expectations, review the process—do not abandon a worthwhile effort—doing so leads only to further failures and declining expectations.

Application of These Ideas

The most significant ideas in this chapter for me were:

_____

As a result, I intend to:

_____

> *This completes the outline of the Seven Best Practices. The*
> *next section will assist you with a list of steps to organize*
> *your ideas and intentions into a doable action plan to*
> *implement the knowledge you have now gained.*

*How a Multi-national Corporation
adapted the Seven Best Practices to train
1,000 supervisors and managers.*

Chapter 10

How a Multi-National Corporation Adapted the Seven Best Practices to Train 1,000 Supervisors and Managers

Introduction

This chapter outlines how a large organization used the Seven Best Practice process and what they did to maximize results, both tangible and intangible.

To protect the confidentiality of this client we simply refer to the name as "ZPX" and inform you that they are a manufacturing entity with more than a 50 plants in the USA, plus several in Canada, Mexico, Europe and Asia. Their market is highly competitive and they constantly search for methods that are likely to generate a competitive edge.

This information is structured in terms of each of the Seven Best Practices to assist you in relating this content to what you have read throughout the book. To speed your reading we have shortened the Seven Best Practices phrase to 7BP and the letters GS refer to Greg Schinkel who was the lead trainer/facilitator.

BP 1: Empower a Leadership Development Team

At ZPX the CEO and executives had discussed and agreed that the organization's most important need was for significant culture change. They confirmed this belief with a formal culture change assessment survey. In measuring the culture it was found to be defensive in nature instead of being constructive. The CEO summed up what he felt was required by saying, "We've never really equipped our front line supervisors and group leaders with the skills they need to effectively lead their people. Most have the technical and operational ability but lack the leadership skills needed in today's workplace."

The director of organizational development was assigned to assemble a team of operational managers to assess what needed to be done, develop a plan and then monitor progress. They were identified as the Development Steering Committee (similar to the Leadership Development Team we recommend.) Several plant managers, three senior executives and the senior vice president of HR were recruited. They were tasked with determining specific actions needed to bring about the desired change, how that would be achieved, preparing the cost estimates and formulating a plan. Fortunately, there was broad agreement that there were many opportunities for improvement.

One of the initial questions they addressed was, "What truly was causing the culture to be the way it was?" They determined that a key element was the supervisors and front line group leaders, who regularly interacted with 95% of the employees on a daily basis. They were the people who most significantly influenced what employees thought and the employee's actions, behaviors and attitudes.

Observations: In this case the Executive Committee acted as the macro steering committee and identified the fundamental need for change. They then tasked the director of organizational development to form the Development Steering Committee that would outline the specifics and formulate the plan and finally ensure that it was successfully carried out.

An interesting aspect was the question they asked themselves early on about what most influenced the behaviors and attitudes of the employee population. Later in this initiative, the same question, but with a twist, was asked this way, "Who influences and impacts the behaviors and attitudes of those same supervisors?" You can no doubt guess that some managers began to feel uncomfortable about the likely answer.

BP 2: Scrutinize the Needs and Opportunities

This is the area where the executives and steering committee members deviated most from the 7BP process. Training needs were routinely identified and discussed prior to setting their annual budgets—but on occasion and in this case the CEO and Executive Committee would delve into operational concerns and what was being planned to deal with them. The training was to be used as the catalyst for culture change through behavior change and all units were expected to participate. Originally the plan was to have 600 people participate but this was expanded to 1,000 because of the extent and range of positive feedback and positive changes in leadership behaviors.

Observations: As the success of this initiative became obvious a decision was made to expand participation. The involvement of senior people at this early stage was even more valuable than expected. It contributed to establishing credibility. It was a major factor in ensuring wide application of the methods and techniques. The involvement of senior management also ensured their buy-in and support and finally it made this project a corporate program and not just an HR training course.

BP 3: Select the trainer/facilitator and methods best able to generate the predetermined gains

ZPX, as you might expect, began their search for qualified training facilitators with a Google search. They specifically searched for the terms, "supervisor training," "lead hand training," "group leader training," and "culture change." This provided a list of consultants/trainers both large and small based in the US, Canada and the UK.

Initial investigation included whether the training organization had experience with manufacturing clients, the names of past clients, and the professionalism of their website. Next they had a member of their team and the director of organizational effectiveness conduct an interview with each of the prospective facilitators. This produced a short list of seven finalists who had some or all of the desired qualifications.

After that they issued a Request for Proposal (RFP) to the seven finalists. While originally they considered enrolling group leaders in the project, they became concerned about the possible cost and so left them out. Again, due to cost concerns, they didn't specify the inclusion of one-on-one coaching and support to help those struggling to apply the methods. Nor did they include follow-up sessions to ensure continuation of the application. The final tally was to train about 600, which included only the first-line supervisors and their managers and only those located in North America. Once the proposals were received each firm was invited to do a presentation at ZPX's headquarters.

Observations: While every step in the process was valuable, this presentation step went beyond providing responses to their RFP. It added new possibilities for improved results and sustainability. It highlighted the scope of what could be done and which firm could likely be most effective. It exposed the degree of preparation and research each training provider had done. It gave the steering committee an opportunity to get a feel for the training approach each would take and how the trainer might relate to ZPX's supervisors.

Some presenters included written support material. The professionalism of this aspect said much about each company. ZPX added coaching sessions for the managers and for the plant managers. There were other elements added that contributed to the outstanding results achieved. The director of organizational effectiveness said, "When we saw the effort and quality of your verbal and written presentations we knew that your firm would do everything needed to ensure success." While that was a major tipping point in their decision to select our firm, the key to clinching the deal was our offer to accept payment of a percentage of our fees based on results achieved using their metrics. It convinced them that we were confident of achieving the desired outcomes.

BP4: Crystallize, focus and communicate– expectations, benefits, indicators and consequences

Of course it all began with the CEO and the Executive Committee. When this group established the scope of what they felt was needed and the importance to the corporation's future success, the die was cast. We know that just because these people say it, doesn't always ensure that it gets done. They have to repeat it many times in many venues. Establishing the Development Steering Committee added to the likelihood of success and what made it most effective was the specific people chosen for this committee: People respected for their knowledge, accomplishments, ability to get things done, and their people skills. In other words they were proven leaders who believed in and were committed to employee development. The very fact that the CEO said all 600 supervisors and managers would participate made a noticeable impact. The more detailed expectations were spelled out as the efforts were launched and implemented.

Observations: We've heard it before, but it bears repeating—low expectations generate low results or no results. What leaders expect, express and exhibit impacts what happens. At ZPX, to their credit, as they saw what was possible they increased their expectations particularly in terms of application and measuring of the outcomes.

BP 5: Launch initiative with dynamic leadership—then monitor progress and take positive action to ensure success

We know that who says what and when affects what gets done. At every location the plant manager and HR manager launched the effort and introduced the facilitator. They were asked to attend the two-day sessions as observers. Unfortunately, because we referred to them as observers they tended to do just that. (Later, we would acknowledge that plant managers and HR managers should have been full participants.) This level of engagement was more comfortable for all and generated a feeling of, "We are going to do this together." To further support the initiative ZPX's CEO regularly reported progress through his quarterly company-wide communications.

Prior to beginning the training, the Development Steering Committee and our president discussed what metrics would be used to judge progress and the final degree of success. All realized that many factors influence operational metrics, but the plant managers would be in the best position to determine if the training was having any positive impact on operations.

The local HR manager was tasked with preparing and submitting a scorecard each month to the plant manager and to GS as the lead trainer. It listed every participant from that location, the dates they attended the training and whether they had submitted documented evidence of their application of course content. The plant manager was required to read the summary of the participant's application journals and meet with GS by telephone each month to review the results. This was much appreciated because the plant manager could see the difference between those who were fluffing their journal entries. He knew who was serious about the program and who wasn't.

Despite using these numerical operational indicators, another proved to be extremely powerful. That was word of mouth, carried by the grapevine. As might be expected, some plant managers and some department managers were enthusiastic supporters and used the opportunity to move continuous improvement and other projects forward. Others were more hesitant and slow in agreeing to participate. We simply suggested they enroll two or three of their people and let them assess the value of the content. Invariably the rave reviews convinced the doubters to check it out for themselves and then they became more than believers, they became promoters of the course. Further they experienced the value and were able to use that to focus on particular initiatives and desired behaviors with each of the supervisors they enrolled. It took on a life of its own.

The director of organizational development commented, "This is amazing, we have never had a training course where people asked to be involved and it's obviously because of what they've heard from others."

Observations: The degree of initial acceptance and enthusiasm was directly in relation to the degree of input and involvement that each plant manager had in the development and shaping of the content and methods. When people experience great and useful training they tell others and support the efforts. This more than anything else determines the overall success of the initiative. (When training is being poorly done, this news too travels the grapevine.)

Pay attention to operational metrics. While there are many factors other than the training that impact them, they do get the attention of line managers. Be wary of trainers who say you can't expect results or that they can't be measured. Although training is rarely used as an assessment tool, it is an indicator of effort and initiative. Ultimately the plant manager at each facility had to reflect on whether the operating measures were positively impacted either that month or as the sessions went on. Both GS and the director of organizational effectiveness recognized that the first month is often too early to tell. By the second month they noticed some positive changes and by the third month they could point to specific operating measures that were improving. In addition, the corporation was meeting its cash flow targets and seeing improvements in productivity and quality and reductions in waste.

BP 6: Celebrate enthusiastically, affirm achievements then—record and report the gains

All too often training in some firms ends on a down note instead of celebration. This is a serious flaw in the leadership practices of those in management and HR who allow it to happen. Of course there are obstacles in some situations, but there are also solutions. In this case, one obstacle was the fact that due to scheduling requirements, some people couldn't participate and graduate until weeks or months after others. So people would graduate in waves and that had a favorable peer pressure effect at the plant level. Stragglers felt more obligated to complete the application journals and the coaching conversations. Plant managers also didn't want to be seen as lagging behind.

The way that successful completion was recognized varied. Many plants hosted a luncheon where the plant manager presented the course graduates with certificates. Usually he/she would express appreciation for the effort and highlight the impact on productivity and on teamwork. Finally, there would be comments about this not being an event but a continuing process of learning and growth.

The completion certificates were impressive and framed and therefore valued. The CEO mentioned successes in the quarterly communications video and tied his comments into the goals which were not only to have operating performance improvement which occurred during the project but also that it was having a positive impact on the culture.

Observations: ZPX did several things right by celebrating the graduation of each participant with enthusiasm. Having the CEO keep the visibility of the initiative front and center over the entire time period helped people realize this was not a flavor-of-the-month program.

BP 7: Refine and repeat the process for culture change, sustainability and competitive advantage

Refining the content and methods began immediately after the first group of 20 participants and the Development Steering Committee attended the pilot program. Scrutinizing all aspects was nerve wracking but the feedback was useful to all involved. What became obvious was that by being sensitive and responsive to the suggestions of so many in the initial design, they realized that we had put too much information into the program. To do everything they said they wanted was not practical in a two-day course. In response, one significant revision was made after the pilot and another about half way through the deployment. Both the materials and training agenda were altered. The refinement continued periodically as 50 groups (more than 1,000 people) completed the course. Each revision was to increase focus on those key areas of greatest need and significance.

Some plants on their own initiative wanted to expand the training to include all employees. The plant managers at these locations felt the trickle down method of changing the organization had its merits... and its limitations. They found that greater gains could be achieved faster by including the employees themselves instead of relying solely on the supervisors and managers to change their leadership approach.

About halfway through the training deployment, they again repeated the culture survey and the results already began to show some improvement. They asked GS which plants seemed to be taking the course more seriously and making serious effort to encourage not only participation but application. They correlated the feedback from GS with the culture survey scores. Not surprisingly they saw a correlation between those plants making serious and determined efforts and those with the best culture improvements.

However, as a company overall there were disappointments as well. While some operations were improving, some seemed to show no improvement and a few got worse. After considering all factors they came to realize that it is unrealistic to achieve culture change with one two-day course.

To their immense credit, they were tenacious. Instead of abandoning the project, they discussed its merits and reconfirmed its value and their determination to forge ahead. They pulled together a new group of different plant managers, different executives and HR people. It was somewhat like the initial Development Steering Team but with a different composition and without vested ownership. Their assignment was to review progress and determine what was and wasn't working. What they learned was that there were factors other than the supervisor's influence and skills that was impacting culture.

While they supported the training activities they had little time to personally relate to their supervisors. Once again they found that those managers who were able to carve out the time in the workday simply to circulate and talk to their people were achieving the better climate survey scores. Another change was to select some plants for what they referred to as, "Intensive Care." They interviewed all of the employees especially to determine what additional factors were significant. Based on this deep dive a Phase 2 to the development program is currently being developed.

The next phase of leadership development will include a specific session for each plant's management team, followed by regional sessions for supervisors focused on fewer topics, delivered in greater depth. Many plant managers expressed their own needs for development and felt that the way they were managed lacked a focus on positive reinforcement. Their regular operational reviews focused almost exclusively on "red items," or problem areas with very little acknowledgment of gains being achieved. With these insights in hand the new steering team identified the need to include executives in the second phase of the training.

There was also acknowledgment that the supervisors were so overloaded with tasks and requirements, they had less time to be personable with employees. So the company looked at how to re-align the responsibilities to allow for more interpersonal contact between supervisors and employees.

Finally, this has created an understanding that rather than using only an external resource, there is a need to involve more of their internal resources. Truly transforming the culture will require a coordinated effort. What they have discovered is that continuous improvement and lean manufacturing are productive and excellent initiatives. However, their contribution is limited without leadership excellence.

Observations: Canned programs are limited in their effectiveness. Every course must have some degree of tailoring to the needs of the participants and the goals of the organization. The greater the level of customization, the greater the perceived relevance and credibility by managers and participants. This leads to greater acceptance, application and achievement by all. An important element in this success was the fact that GS visited several plants, talked to plant managers and HR people, developed the design and conducted most of the training. This deep involvement facilitated the adjustments to more closely fit the needs and preferences of plant managers and enabled him to make meaningful suggestions to the HR people.

It is always a challenge to attempt to pack everything everyone has ever wanted into a single training program. Those leading the efforts must focus on what is both most relevant and most useful to the participants.

One of the keys here was the measurement, the listening to all involved and the willingness to adapt and make changes. This responsiveness is soon evident and appreciated by all. Avoid restricting those who want to move faster and don't delay progress waiting for laggards. Keep at it despite setbacks, delays and resistance. Those are to be expected. Determine the causes, make needed changes, recruit supporters and move forward relentlessly. If the goals are still significant keep at it and get it done.

You now know the Seven Best Practices. You have read the stories about how the process has been used in small and medium size companies and how they have benefitted. Now you have seen how a multi-national, multi-location corporation used the same basic methods. At this point you need to decide what you are going to do with this knowledge, how will you apply it and learn from that experience; how you can use this information to benefit the organization you are with and how you can help the people and leaders in it grow in skill, confidence and success.

Keep in mind that you don't have to try and do this alone. Every one of these organizations and hundreds more like them have called on assistance from Greg and his associates.

The next chapter has been written to provide some basic steps to help you get started.

Chapter 11

Pursue the Possibilities and Potential

Check your personal commitment
Assess the situation
Identify resources available
Outline the benefits for key stakeholders
Do a reality check
Recruit positive allies
Target doable opportunities in their areas
Keep at it everlastingly—until you succeed!

Reason: A well-conceived plan provides a starting point, a path to follow and generates confidence.

INSPIRE

You will never process what you are unwilling to pursue.

–Mike Murdock

You miss 100% of the shots you don't take.

–Hockey Legend Wayne Gretzky

Chapter 11

Plan, Prepare and Pursue the Possibilities and the Potential

A well conceived plan provides a starting point, a path to follow and generates confidence.

The ultimate purpose of every organization—its mission—is to supply a product or service that satisfies the needs and wants of its customers/clients at a competitive cost.

The purpose of every employee's responsibility is to contribute to this mission in some specific way, adding value to the product or service that is supplied to the end customer.

The purpose of the human resources and the training function is to provide the advice, counseling, knowledge, and skills required. Their purpose is also to assist managers in coaching and mentoring skills, which enables application and improved outcomes.

Increasingly, Unit Leaders are asking department heads and their people two simple and direct questions:

1. "How does what you do add value to what we supply to our customers/clients?

2. Give me three examples of how you have done that."

Unrealized Potential Exists Everywhere

Where do we begin to identify unrealized potential? First, know that it exists everywhere. A few examples should help in understanding this phenomenon:

In the chapter "Best Practices Two" the United Way story demonstrates that by taking the best that has been proven possible in one area and utilizing it in other areas will provide a goal. The gap between the best and the current level is unrealized potential. Often the difference is enormous and extremely valuable. However, in other instances a miniscule improvement of 1% or 2% is significant because of the large volumes involved.

Back in chapter five, the lube and grease sales representatives at Nationwide were achieving a certain level of gross profit margin. After sales training, role-play and coaching by the facilitator and their sales manager, they were able to increase the profit margin substantially, and reduced the unrealized potential. Training was the catalyst and enabler.

Similarly, in virtually every anecdote in the book, we see that problems are always opportunities for improvement. Any change can also be a catalyst for gains. However, every action requires a leader—a champion—a person with initiative. You can be that person.

Start Now

An ending is always a new beginning. At this point, you have gained insights into the benefits that can be achieved through using leadership development to leverage progress. You can decide, "Well that's interesting and maybe someday I will do something about it," which makes the time you spent in reading the book of limited value. Or, you can decide now that you will take steps to implement these ideas and begin the journey to greater gains.

> **For some, the urge to go forward is dampened by doubts. The vision of achieving great gains is obscured by a fog of imagined "what if" barriers. There is a teeter-totter in our minds; at one end are doubts, at the other end is determination.**

A business owner once shared this type of hesitation saying, "I had resigned my sales job with a major business forms company and was equipped to start my own business. The business cards and letterhead were printed. The small office was rented and the telephone connected. I was ready for customers. I even decided that I would start soliciting customers door to door in the business area nearby starting the following Monday at 9:30 AM. When the day arrived, I parked the car, then stood for an hour deciding which side of the street to start on." Of course he finally did start, and one customer at a time he developed a thriving business.

> **The point is that we are often delayed**
> **by doubts when there truly are no**
> **obstacles but our own uncertainties.**

Therefore, develop a simple plan to help get you started and so dispel any doubts and double your determination.

Step One: Summarize the Current Situation

Begin by summarizing the current situation as you see it by circling the appropriate responses below:

1. How committed to training and development is your organization now?

   High   Medium   Low

2. Does the Unit Leader demonstrate interest and support for leadership development?

   Often   Occasionally   Seldom

3. Have training initiatives been effective in the past?

   Often   Somewhat   Not At All   Uncertain

4. How capable, committed and energized do you feel right now?

   Very   Somewhat   Not At All

What would be most helpful in building **your** confidence?

   ____ Additional information

   ____ Advice from an external source

   ____ Observing and teaming- up with an external facilitator

   ____ Other (Please describe) _____

Step Two: Review Your Application Notes

While reading this book, you were encouraged to make notes. For this step review them in the following manner:

On one page list what you feel needs to be done:

1. Prioritize what needs to happen, and in what sequence, by:

   a. Those you can readily implement yourself.

   b. Those you can implement with approval.

   c. Those requiring the co-operation and/or support of others.

2. List how these would benefit the organization, and the various stakeholders.

3. Summarize how this would contribute to the organization's performance and, that magic word "profitability" (or better, faster, cheaper.)

Step Three: List Potential Obstacles

It is always best to identify the potential obstacles to success. The following will assist you. List potential barriers below:

For each, show at least three possible solutions. Beside each, note whether the perceived obstacle is:

External (Systemic, procedural, resources or other people), or
Internal (Your own mindset, perceptions, knowledge or doubts)

Potential Obstacle	External/Internal	Possible Solutions

Step Four: Consider Available Resources

Expand your mind to consider all possible available resources. Here are a few examples:

1. Consider associates who are enthusiastic, capable and supportive.

2. Use this book. This can help others understand what you propose to achieve, the methods and the potential gains.

3. The authors and facilitators at Unique Training & Development Inc. who can be of value by:

   - Teaming with you to do a presentation for key people.

   - Assisting you and/or others in a readiness review.

   - Consulting in a variety of areas.

   - Assisting with a pilot effort enabling you and others to learn from the experience.

   - Delivering high quality training workshops.

Step Five: Develop a Plan

Be crisp and precise in developing your plan of action. These suggestions have proven effective:

- **Determine readiness and receptivity** by "walking around." Talk to those people whom you know to be most receptive to new ideas. Ask them about those elements which have been listed on the first pages of the first two chapters in this book (Training Well Done and Training Not Done.)

  a. Listen for difficulties and issues which now or could possibly effect the products or services supplied to your customers/clients.

- **Develop an "elevator" pitch.** A summary of what you propose, and the potential benefits. It should be brief enough to be communicated in about 90 seconds. The purpose is to inform and generate interest.

- **Inform them** that you are looking to recruit one or two Unit Leaders to test the methods. The criteria for selecting these potential leaders is as follows:

  a. Those interested in innovation, improvement and tangible results.

  b. Enthusiastic leaders with a positive, action oriented, can-do attitude.

  c. Those who relate well to people and have the ability to gain their support.

  d. Leaders committed to pursuing potential sustainability.

  e. Those willing to record and communicate both successes and setbacks and share those experiences with others so everyone learns.

- **Consider one or two target areas** that are doable. Choose those that are likely to be successful and have support, and where the results can readily be measured.

- **Recommend the formation of a Leadership Development Team** and actively pursue approval. Campaign personally in order to influence management towards a favorable decision. (If this is unlikely to happen, do what you can do with those most favorably inclined to support this action.)

- **Follow the Seven Best Practices relentlessly.**

The following form is a document for use now or in future titled "Training Gains: Planning and Reporting." By using this format, you are guided through the Seven Step Process for each scheduled initiative.

Training Gains: Planning and Reporting

List Leadership Development Team members contributing input and support: _____

_____

Training needs and priorities based on potential contribution to areas of:

Support for strategic organizational goals: _____

_____

To seize problem/opportunities as follows: _____

_____

To develop executive, management, supervisor and employee skills:

_____

Training program selected title:_____

Reason selected:_____

Trainer/facilitator(s) selected name(s):_____

      Internal: _____ External: _____

      Reasons for choice:_____

Expectations to be communicated by the Unit Leader:

    a. To participants by:_____

    b. To line managers by:_____

    c. To human resources by:_____

    d. To trainer/facilitator by:_____

    e. Oversight to ensure action will be provided by:

      _____

Program launch: will be on:_____it will be done by:_____

    a. Progress monitoring and reporting will be done by:

    _____

    b. Mentoring and coaching of participants will be done by:

    _____

    c. Corrective action if required will be done by:_____

Celebration event: will be held on:_____Organized by:_____

    a. Results (Tangible and intangible) will be accumulated and reported by:_____

    b. Input will be provided by line managers with reference to related indicators: _____

Refine and repeat: the process and plan for continuity and sustainability. A debriefing meeting will be held on:_____

Chaired by:_____

Members of the Leadership Development
Team will individually have input.

The Bottom-Line

	Costs Estimated:	Costs Actual:
1. Trainer/facilitator fees	_____	_____
2. Participant materials	_____	_____
3. Facilities & equipment	_____	_____
4. Celebration expense	_____	_____
5. Participant costs:	_____	_____
a. Travel expenses	_____	_____
b. Accommodation	_____	_____
6. Other	_____	_____
Totals:		

Gains Achieved: Tangible Indicators

1. Once only gains: _____

2. Continuing gains: _____

3. Cascading gains: _____

4. Spontaneous discoveries: _____

5. Intangible gains (Behavior changes): _____

In Summary

Learning and progress accrue only when there is something to learn from, and that something, the stuff of learning and progress, is any completed action.

A powerful new idea can kick around unused in a company for years, not because its merits are not recognized, but because nobody has assumed the responsibility for converting it from words into action. Ideas are useless unless used.

> ★ It's just amazing what a handful of dedicated people
>   can do when they are really turned on.
>
> *INSPIRE*
>
> *– In Search of Excellence by Peters and Waterman*

In the Introduction a golf example was used and it seems fitting to offer another for this closing page.

Lorne Rubenstein wrote an article about his experiences in attempting to improve his golf handicap. Over time he received instruction and advice from such greats as Tom Watson, Chuck Cook, Patti McGowan, Jack Grout and Moe Norman among others. All of this advice had little effect on his numbers. Then one day at The Medalist Golf Club in Hobe Sound Florida, Bob Toski the first inductee into the World Golf Teachers Hall of Fame, yelled out, "Stop thinking. Just hit the damn ball." That was great advice!

Never wait for conditions to be perfect.

Begin where you are now.

Replace doubts with determination.

Use what you already know.

Go in the direction you have chosen.

Access the resources available and
make the best progress possible.

Learn and adjust as you go.

Ultimately and inevitably you will reach your goal!

INSPIRE

The method of the enterprising is to plan
with audacity and execute with vigor.

–*John Christian Bovee*

The Final Word!
'Perseverando'
(Latin)

Appreciation

Our Clients, Thank you for the opportunities we have had to work with you and your staff. Those experiences and insights form the anecdotes offered in this book. They will assist others in living and understanding the situations, solutions and results. We are grateful for the interactions that have allowed us to be a part of your lives and challenges.

Jeff Keenor's disciplined approach as an electrical engineer and former general manager of a division in a corporate situation was most helpful. His frustration with the original draft and detailed suggestions drove us to make needed major improvements.

Dick Cochrill's combination of experience as an independent business owner, as a consultant for Ontario Skills Development and more recently as director of a non-profit organization was unique. This broad viewpoint encouraged us to expand the applicability of the content.

Doug Dolman contributed his experiences not only as a vice president in a national financial organization but a moving personal experience. In this instance he was invited to take part as a guest resource at an executive development retreat. The eagerness and sincerity of the participants made an impression that lives with him still.

Steve Jones joined our company as a facilitator after a lengthy career in the food industry. While there he personally felt and saw the effectiveness of one of our courses. Several of the situations described in the material were his contributions.

Jim Kehoe reviewed the "numbers" in the anecdotes and suggested changes to improve reader understanding and ensure conformance to accepted accounting terminology.

Deborah Dunn-Roy and Carl Roy shared their observations regarding leadership, training, communications, and budgeting in the health-care field.

"Bud" Edwards completed the final read-through of the manuscript and found a few of those pesky errors that seem never-ending. As a former principal/administrator, he shared observations regarding the education field. Similar to training, there is a need to find more effective methods and relate content to application.

Lori Vos, a senior tutor at Queens University's Writing Centre helped with answers as we neared completion.

Kathy Glover Scott, our editor, helped us to organize and present our ideas and experience in a way that is easier to understand and apply.

Gwen Gades for interior book design. Purple Penguin Book Design and Coaching.

Cathi Stevenson at Book Cover Express for the cover design. Over numerous projects, Cathi's keen eye for design has created covers that "pop."

Jaclyn Bierbaum, no we didn't forget you. Thanks for inputting information from barely legible notes and for being there.

About The Authors

Irwin Schinkel early in his career participated in a course that sparked an enduring interest in training and its powerful influence. He saw participants grow in terms of their personality, confidence and enthusiasm.

Subsequently, although holding management positions in marketing and human resources, with two divisions of the world's largest automaker, his extra-curricular activities were often devoted to developing others. These ranged from sales training in Trinidad and the Barbados to management training for a variety of businesses and industries to an extension course in organizational development for Western University.

Finally, his passion led him to leave the corporate world and establish Unique Training & Development. After a decade Greg Schinkel acquired the company and Irwin now devotes his time to writing and world travel. He and his wife Jan live in Ontario, Canada and Florida, USA.

Greg Schinkel has established himself as an expert in developing front line supervisors, managers and team leaders to increase productivity and maximize employee involvement and motivation.

Having reached more than 500,000 people through his writing, speaking, training, television and radio appearances, Greg is known for adapting his approach and terminology with his clients. He is sought after as a management consultant, trainer, keynote speaker and coach for his unique blend of style and substance.

Since graduating from the prestigious Richard Ivey School of Business, Greg has served as chapter president of the Canadian Association of Professional Speakers and the Canadian Association of Family Enterprise. He has served as president of the Rotary Club of London, Canada. Greg also co-authored this book and a previous book titled, *Employees Not Doing What You Expect*, which has been published on three continents. He wrote the book *What Great Supervisors Know* and was a contributing author to *Awakening the Workplace*.

Join thousands of other subscribers who receive Greg's free Leader Feeder newsletter and the practical insights it offers. Simply visit: UniqueDevelopment.com. In addition, for free useful forms visit our site for this book: FusionorFizzle.com. Several videos are available at UniqueTrainingVideos.com.

Quotable Quotes

"Beware of good; it is often a barrier to better and best."

"Leaders tend to get what they expect, express and exhibit."

"Credentials do not guarantee capability, commitment or character."

"There is a teeter-totter in most minds. At one end sits doubt at the other determination."

"We are often delayed by doubts when there truly are no obstacles but our own uncertainties."

"Never wait for conditions to be perfect.
Instead, begin where you are now.
Replace doubts with determination.
Use what you already know.
Go in the direction you have chosen.
Access the resources available and
make the best progress possible.
Learn and adjust as you go.
Ultimately and inevitably—
you will reach your goal!"

"There are impressive gains available in many organizations, untapped because of a negative focus only on costs and budgets rather than on pursuit of potential gains. Some leaders, inadvertently and unintentionally limit the success of their people and their organization by this mindset."

"Criticism no matter how well intended, delivered or deserved, will foster a natural tendency to distort, or deny, or minimize problems— thereby foiling their elimination and the gains that could accrue."

Suggested Reading

Analyzing Performance Problems by Robert Mager & Peter Pipe

Awakening the Workplace by Greg Schinkel et al

Employees Not Doing What You Expect ... Find Out Why Fix It, Prevent It in Future Turn Negative Situations into Positive Relationships by Greg Schinkel and Irwin Schinkel

What Great Supervisors Know by Greg Schinkel

Good To Great by Jim Collins

Switch: How to Change Things When Change Is Hard by Chip and Dan Heath

In Search of Excellence by Peters & Waterman

Managing from the Heart by Bracey, Rosenblum, Sanford and Trueblood

Quality is Free by Philip Crosby

Thriving on Chaos by Tom Peters

What Got You Here Won't Get You There by Marshall Goldsmith

Winning by Jack Welch

Words That Change Minds by Shelle Rose Charvet

Resource Order Form

Four easy ways to order:

1. **Fax orders:** (519)685-9043 using this form

2. **Telephone orders:** Call (866)700-9043 toll free, or (226) 777-0147.
   ### Please have your credit card ready

3. **Email orders:** orders@uniquedevelopment.com

4. **Online orders:** UniqueDevelopment.com

   - Please send me _____ additional copies of *Fusion or Fizzle* @ $19.95 CDN or $19.95 U.S. + S&H

   - I'm interested in purchasing more than 5 copies of the book. Please send information regarding volume discounts.

   - Begin my FREE subscription to the Leader Feeder Newsletter

   - Provide additional information about: _____

Name:_____

Address:_____

City:_____ **State/Prov:**_____

Zip/PC:_____**Telephone:**_____

Email:_____

Sales Tax: Please add 5% GST for products shipped to Canadian address.

Shipping by Air: Canada/USA $7.00 for first book and $4.00 for each additional product.

International: $15.00 for first book and $7.00 for each additional product.

PAYMENT:

VISA   Mastercard   Amex   Cheque/Money Order

Card Number:_____

Name on Card:_____

Exp.Date:_____SecurityCode:_____

Signature:_____

Index

["

www.ingramcontent.com/pod-product-compliance
Lightning Source LLC
Chambersburg PA
CBHW070716220326
41598CB00024BA/3175